▶ **Screen Distribution and the New King Kongs of the Online World**

DOI: 10.1057/9781137326454

Other Palgrave Pivot titles

Nevenko Bartulin: Honorary Aryans: National–Racial Identity and Protected Jews in the Independent State of Croatia

Coreen Davis: State Terrorism and Post-transitional Justice in Argentina: An Analysis of Mega Cause I Trial

Deborah Lupton: The Social Worlds of the Unborn

Shelly McKeown: Identity, Segregation and Peace-Building in Northern Ireland: A Social Psychological Perspective

Rita Sakr: 'Anticipating' the 2011 Arab Uprisings: Revolutionary Literatures and Political Geographies

Timothy Jenkins: Of Flying Saucers and Social Scientists: A Re-Reading of When Prophecy Fails and of Cognitive Dissonance

Ben Railton: The Chinese Exclusion Act: What It Can Teach Us about America

Patrick Joseph Ryan: Master-Servant Childhood: A History of the Idea of Childhood in Medieval English Culture

Andrew Dowdle, Scott Limbocker, Song Yang, Karen Sebold, and Patrick A. Stewart: Invisible Hands of Political Parties in Presidential Elections: Party Activists and Political Aggregation from 2004 to 2012

Jean-Paul Gagnon: Evolutionary Basic Democracy: A Critical Overture

Mark Casson and Catherine Casson: The Entrepreneur in History: From Medieval Merchant to Modern Business Leader

Tracy Shilcutt: Infantry Combat Medics in Europe, 1944–45

Asoka Bandarage: Sustainability and Well-Being: The Middle Path to Environment, Society, and the Economy

Panos Mourdoukoutas: Intelligent Investing in Irrational Markets

Jane Wong Yeang Chui: Affirming the Absurd in Harold Pinter

Carol L. Sherman: Reading Olympe de Gouges

Elana Wilson Rowe: Russian Climate Politics: When Science Meets Policy

Joe Atikian: Industrial Shift: The Structure of the New World Economy

Tore Bjørgo: Strategies for Preventing Terrorism

Kevin J. Burke, Brian S. Collier and Maria K. McKenna: College Student Voices on Educational Reform: Challenging and Changing Conversations

Raphael Sassower: Digital Exposure: Postmodern Postcapitalism

Peter Taylor-Gooby: The Double Crisis of the Welfare State and What We Can Do About It

Jeffrey Meyers: Remembering Iris Murdoch: Letter and Interviews

Grace Ji-Sun Kim: Colonialism, *Han*, and the Transformative Spirit

Rodanthi Tzanelli: Olympic Ceremonialism and the Performance of National Character: From London 2012 to Rio 2016

Marvin L. Astrada and Félix E. Martín: Russia and Latin America: From Nation-State to Society of States

Ramin Jahanbegloo: Democracy in Iran

Mark Chou: Theorising Democide: Why and How Democracies Fail

DOI: 10.1057/9781137326454

palgrave▶pivot

Screen Distribution and the New King Kongs of the Online World

Stuart Cunningham

and

Jon Silver

DOI: 10.1057/9781137326454

First published 2013 by
PALGRAVE MACMILLAN

Palgrave Macmillan in the UK is an imprint of Macmillan Publishers Limited, registered in England, company number 785998, of Houndmills, Basingstoke, Hampshire RG21 6XS.

Palgrave Macmillan in the US is a division of St Martin's Press LLC, 175 Fifth Avenue, New York, NY 10010.

Palgrave Macmillan is the global academic imprint of the above companies and has companies and representatives throughout the world.

Palgrave® and Macmillan® are registered trademarks in the United States, the United Kingdom, Europe and other countries

ISBN: 978-1-137-32646-1 EPUB
ISBN: 978-1-137-32645-4 PDF
ISBN: 978-1-137-32644-7 Hardback

This book is printed on paper suitable for recycling and made from fully managed and sustained forest sources. Logging, pulping and manufacturing processes are expected to conform to the environmental regulations of the country of origin.

A catalogue record for this book is available from the British Library.

A catalog record for this book is available from the Library of Congress.

DOI: 10.1057/9781137326454

Contents

DOI: 10.1057/9781137326454

List of Tables

DOI: 10.1057/9781137326454

Acknowledgements

We thank Adam Swift for his expert research assistance, Mark Ryan and John McDonnell for early collaborations, and Michael Keane and Elaine Zhao for their assistance with the China case study. We thank Felicity Plester and Chris Penfold at Palgrave Macmillan, and the anonymous readers of our proposal and manuscript, for their encouragement and assistance.

Some material in this book has been revised from a couple of earlier publications and used with permission: Cunningham, Stuart, Silver, Jon and McDonnell, John. 2010. "Rates of change: online distribution as disruptive technology in the film industry." *Media International Australia* 136: 119–132; Cunningham, Stuart and Silver, Jon. 2012. "Online film distribution: its history and global complexion." In *Digital disruption: cinema moves online*, edited by Dina Iordanova and Stuart Cunningham, 33–66. St Andrews: St Andrews Film Studies; and Silver, Jon, Cunningham, Stuart and Ryan, Mark D. 2012. "Mission Unreachable: how Jaman is shaping the future of on-line distribution." In *Digital Disruption: Cinema Moves Online*, edited by Dina Iordanova and Stuart Cunningham, 133–142. St Andrews: St Andrews Film Studies.

The Authors

Stuart Cunningham is Distinguished Professor of Media and Communications, Queensland University of Techology, and Director of the Australian Research Council Centre of Excellence for Creative Industries and Innovation. He is one of Australia's most prominent media scholars. His recent work includes *Hidden Innovation: Policy, Industry and the Creative Sector* (2013), *Key Concepts in Creative Industries* (with John Hartley, Jason Potts, Terry Flew, John Banks, and Michael Keane, 2013), and *Digital Disruption: Cinema Moves On-line* (edited with Dina Iordanova, 2012).

Jon Silver is Senior Lecturer in Film, Television and Digital Media, Creative Industries Faculty, Queensland University of Technology. His research focuses on strategic issues facing the screen content businesses. A key focus is on the impacts of new technology on distribution and exhibition. He has worked in senior executive roles in film production, distribution, and exhibition.

DOI: 10.1057/9781137326454

List of Abbreviations

DECE	Digital Entertainment Content Ecosystem
DTHT	Direct to Home Television
DTO	download-to-own
EST	electronic sell through
FTTH	Fibre to the Home
IP	Internet Protocol
IPTV	Internet Protocol TV
MPA	Motion Picture Association (of America)
OTT	over-the-top
OS	Operating System
P2P	Peer-to-Peer
PPV	Pay Per View
pro–am	professional–amateur
ROW	rest of the world
SARFT	State Administration of Radio, Film and Television
SVOD	Subscription Video on Demand
TOD	Theatre on Demand
UGC	user-generated content
VOD	Video on Demand

palgrave▶**pivot**

www.palgrave.com/pivot

Introduction

Abstract: *In seeking to understand the great changes that are happening to screen distribution as major new players enter the market, this book refrains from engaging in the predictable wild optimism or dour pessimism that usually accompanies such discussions. We outline a "middle range" theoretical framework and employ a "middle way" cultural politics that shows the reality is more complex and open to opportunity. We argue that only very recently are we beginning to see the new online distribution giants starting to operate as TV-like networks. By exploring this stage, we are able to analyse the rate at which change is occurring, how this change impacts business models and organisational cultures, and what value can be placed on these changes.*

Keywords: media and communications studies; online distribution; screen distribution; film distribution; future of television; middle range theory

Cunningham, Stuart and Silver, Jon. *Screen Distribution and the New King Kongs of the Online World*. Basingstoke: Palgrave Macmillan, 2013. DOI: 10.1057/9781137326454.

Ever since the first online VOD platform, IFilm, launched in 1997, there has been intense and ongoing debate about the likely impacts of new technologies and convergence on screen distribution. For proponents of "digital democracy", the ubiquity of affordable, high-quality production and post-production equipment combined with the ability to digitise screen content and then leverage the Internet to push that content to a broad audience had the potential to radically alter the way in which film and television programs are created and distributed. And in doing so, the potential to sell direct to individual consumers or niche or mass audiences could undermine the longstanding distribution dominance of the world's major media companies ("The Majors") as happened in the decimation of the music business in only a few short years. Others countered that as barriers to entry were lowered by new technologies, "The Majors" would move to defend their turf and would re-affirm their dominance because they had the size and scale and motivation to deploy the necessary resources in order to maintain their market power. The 21st century truly unleashed the digital genie but, depending on one's point-of-view, the departing genie left a bottle either half full or half empty.

In this book we argue that, unlike the music business or newspapers and book publishing, new technologies have had a slower impact in screen distribution. In Chapter 1, we identify three waves of emergent "market leaders" in the online space for the distribution of film and television programs. During the first stage of the new online distribution industry (from 1997–2002), pioneering firms like IFilm, Atom Films, Intertainer, SightSound, CinemaNow were small, under-capitalised and ahead of their time. The technology and the market was not yet ready for these innovators. They quickly disappeared – either acquired by larger firms or went broke. In the four-stage industry lifecycle theory – fragmentation–shakeout–maturity–decline (McGahan et al. 2004) following the pioneering fragmentation stage is the shakeout, when mergers and acquisitions are common and larger firms emerge as market leaders ready to dominate the industry during the mature stage. The shakeout began around 2001 when the Hollywood Majors moved into the online distribution space – driven mainly by fear and trying to avoid a fate similar to their corporate siblings when the major music companies were challenged fundamentally by peer-to-peer file sharing. Six movie studios launched two major VOD sites in 2001: Movielink (originally branded MovieFly), a joint-venture between Sony, Paramount, Universal, MGM-UA and Warner; and Moviebeam

DOI: 10.1057/9781137326454

(Disney). However, a mass audience willing to pay for legal film and TV content online did not yet exist and they failed to establish viable business models. By 2004–2005, both were sold to third parties for much less than their set up costs.

As the shakeout stage progressed, the third wave of major players in this online distribution space began emerging from the mid-2000s – Apple's iTunes, Netflix, Amazon and Hulu and they remain market leaders to the present.

The key lesson in this tale, until quite recently, is when it comes to the sale or rental of film and television programming to online audiences, Hollywood content, as the saying famously goes, has been king. There was, until recently, little evidence of a critical mass of online viewers willing to pay for alternative fare – smaller independent films or non-Hollywood content – or major on-line platforms willing to invest in backing such fare. The exceptions have been Bollywood films and the eager consumers of the global Indian and subcontinental diaspora and other lovers of the style. Chapter 2 scans the global field, noting the number of smaller, independent online distribution sites that have failed or are still battling to find a workable niche online. What is definitely brewing, however, outside Hollywood, and Silicon Valley and its epigones, is what is happening to video content online in China. The merger of two giant YouTube clones – Youku and Tudou – will dominate the enormous Chinese cultural space and through its sheer scale and ambition will exert global influence.

We conclude that right now, the fires of creative destruction are still burning and online distribution remains in the shakeout stage as sufficient viewers willing to pay for content develops critical mass online and major platforms begin to invest non-trivial effort into new models of engagement and funding into new content. The stabilisation of this process, according to classical theory (McGahan et al. 2004), will begin to see online distribution entering an early stage of maturity, and an emerging oligopoly of dominant firms whose profitability may also begin to stabilise. We propose that this stage is now approaching and that the composition of an online distribution oligopoly is now predictable. We also contend that companies within this emerging online oligopoly, by design, are likely to emerge as the first global online television "networks" and it is these interests that will have to answer the key question: how is screen content going to be paid for sustainably into the future? (Chapter 3 addresses what is entailed in calling the new platforms nascent "TV networks".)

DOI: 10.1057/9781137326454

We also argue that all the evidence points to Hollywood, and the firms that own the major studios, not controlling the online distribution space – this despite numerous millions having been spent trying to do just that. Apple, Amazon, Netflix and Hulu have all been mentioned, but other firms also have the potential to dominate in this space. YouTube, in tandem with its parent company Google, has rapidly emerged since 2009 (as it took its first steps to professionalise its content and lay foundations for reinventing itself as a global television network online) as perhaps the most threatening market challenger to all – incumbents and new players alike. Facebook has thus far dabbled only tentatively in the online video distribution space but has the scale, resources and dedicated user-base to become a serious player in Internet television should it choose to do so and there are some indicators that it might (https://www.facebook.com/notes/fb-teevee/watch-tv-on-facebook-with-fb-teevee/234999919852604; http://fbteevee.com and http://fbteevee.com/compare.php). The financially troubled Yahoo! has invested heavily and enjoyed recent success in creating original content for the Internet or "web originals".

In Chapter 3, we will briefly draw on lessons from two previous periods of film and television history which, we argue, provide analogies to what is happening today. We also bring together a wide variety of industry data – trade press, annual reports, website content analysis and expert blogs – to argue the case that embryonic global television networks are now emerging in the current online distribution environment. This is what Chapters 4 and 5 are about. But Hollywood history is brought to bear to allay fears, given the fast-changing nature of the story we are telling, that we will add to what Tom Streeter calls "the plague of 'presentism' that frames discussions of the Internet in terms of a radical break from the past" (Lee and Streeter 2012, 96). What is going on is a battle in the "attention economy" (Lanham 2006) – a battle for eyeballs – and the corporations best placed to win that battle may not necessarily be the media companies that to-date have dominated the movie and television industries but those firms that control the platforms that deliver content to larger and larger audiences across multiple screens: the "second", "third" and "fourth" screens (TV, computers and mobile devices). (Cinema was first.)

So one of the lessons to be drawn from this may be that, if content is *king*, then distribution is *King Kong*. The power and profitability in screen industries have always resided in distribution. As Jonathan Knee (2011) argues,

DOI: 10.1057/9781137326454

The economic structure of the media business is not fundamentally different from that of business in general. The most-prevalent sources of industrial strength are the mutually reinforcing competitive advantages of scale and customer captivity. Content creation simply does not lend itself to either, while aggregation is amenable to both.

To what extent is the present moment one where we can trace a decoupling of powerful controllers of content supply and those emerging powers which control the new distribution platforms?

In Chapter 6, we ask *how* significant all this change might be. To what extent does having these large corporations increasingly control the flow of digital entertainment content change matters? Some of these corporations work on a very different model of sourcing content – they are "access" corporations and offer a far wider range of opportunities for not only amateur but pro–am and professional content creators. Some of them have pioneered what we call the "IT-innovation" model, as opposed to the "premium content-mass media" model, of pricing and positioning content with respect to its distribution platform and hardware-device delivery, accelerating the long-term movement from premium product to curated services in the audiovisual environment. On the other hand, reference to industry history indicates that, like all large-scale corporations, they are likely to use market power to seek to limit competition and corral users inside walled gardens.

There is some evidence that this presages real change. And that may be good news for independents around the world because the opportunity is there for good content and a sufficient number of more openly accessible video platforms now exist to distribute that content. The potential is there for next generation filmmakers, as long as they grasp the dynamics of social media and the intense feedback loops it creates, to find the right audience online. They don't necessarily need Hollywood or its distributor epigones. Hollywood has its global platform – cinemas and the well-established post-theatrical release-windows pathway. It seeks to maintain its dominance playing an old-world game – controlling the flow of content onto that platform and using blockbuster marketing strategies and wide releases to roadblock access to cinema screens by its competitors. Hollywood will continue to play that game but the major studios have had two opportunities to dominate the Web by controlling the platform – they failed with Movielink and it will not surprise us if the three major networks that own Hulu and are known to be in conflict about what direction it should take following the departure of its founding CEO Jason Kilar, either sell it, dilute its value proposition so that it ceases to pose a threat to the major television networks, or shut it down. The real action of the future will be digital and online. In what form and with what levels of control will the Majors survive longer term?

How to make sense of it all: a middle-range (and middle-way) approach

There is no more central issue in media and communications studies today than the proposition that we are in the middle of a rapid process of change which is seeing established or "old" media being challenged for primacy in audiences' and users' attention by new modes and types of production, dissemination and display. Reworking the famous communications dictum as "what's going on, why, by whom, where and with what effect" is what preoccupies us today.

But the problem is that most debate about industry structure and change in film, media and communication studies, and in critical humanities and social sciences generally, is based on an exaggerated opposition between enthusiastic optimism and determined scepticism over the potential of new technologies. There are assertions of "fundamental crisis" in the strategies of the media and communications industries versus counter assertions of *plus ça change, plus c'est la même chose* – that the present is a minor blip in the march of hegemonic capital.

This is a depressing predicament and inhibits these discipline's claims to providing rigorous insight into industry change which is, after all, continuous. It is based on deep-seated values which often results in "glass-half-empty/glass-half-full" debates which manage the challenging complexity of universes of data by dividing them into selective portions that confirm previously established positions.

At the industry coalface, the reality is much more confused and complex. The long-term decline in newspaper circulation is seemingly irreversible. But there is evidence that some newspapers have managed to maintain their circulations in the face of long-term industry decline. This is usually based on a business model of hard news targeted at specific, upmarket, demographics which may work even in the straightened circumstances of the print media.

DOI: 10.1057/9781137326454

There is surely no doubt that the exponential growth of the blogo-sphere and of amateur or citizen journalism can be a democratising trend, but the equally dramatic loss of employment prospects in "public trust", or "fourth estate" journalism has as much potential for creating a democratic deficit through the loss of experienced journalists from the public sphere.

The music industry has been turned upside down by the ease with which peers can download and share their favourite playlist. Major new players like Apple iTunes and Spotify and Vevo have upturned the music distribution industry – but it remains the case that commercial and communitarian-but-legal options still represent a small minority of the total download and sharing activity via the Net. Even if it hasn't changed fundamentally the culture of piracy, it must be remembered that it took a computer company (albeit with a remarkable record of innovation) to develop a successful download business based on what we will call the "IT-innovation" model. Meanwhile, the recording industry remains bit-terly divided about the legalities of digital consumption, with the majors (Sony-BMG, Warner Music, Universal Music) continuing to claim ongo-ing devastation while other evidence (for example, Handke 2006) points to judicious use of the Net as a promotional medium benefiting most music entrepreneurs. New green business shoots have followed in the wake of such creative destruction.

Change is indeed continuous, but critics tend to over- or under-read it. Are we "both witnesses to and participants in the largest, most fun-damental transformation in the history of the media since the advent of typeface, the moving image, and terrestrial broadcast transmission" (Levin 2009, 258) or is the evidence for the supplanting of old by new "sparse and thin" (Miller 2010, 10) and ignores the way the new is folded into the old, adding to rather than killing it off? In her magisterial work *The Printing Press as an Agent of Change*, Elizabeth Eisenstein (1979) points out that Europe was relatively stable in 1450, before the Gutenberg revolution, and was relatively stable in 1550, after it. But in the interven-ing decades, there was chaos and great change in values and institutions and much experimentation. Historians, she says, have ignored the tran-sitional times.

In the spirit of Eisenstein, we need to ask: as a contribution to "middle-range theory", how do we study the process and the rate of change? In this case of screen distribution, are there new players dis-rupting the established Hollywood oligopoly and, if so, with what effect?

DOI: 10.1057/9781137326454

Is there evidence of disruption to business models? What has really changed if what we are seeing is the changing of the guard from one powerful oligopoly to another? What substance do we accord to trends toward disintermediation, or "bottom-up" access for new content creators to wide distribution potential?

Claims for a "middle-range" approach draws on some important academic forebears. Perhaps the best known are David Bordwell and Noël Carroll, who, in *Post-Theory: Reconstructing Film Studies* (1996), take issue with "grand theories" (post-structuralism, Lacanian psychoanalysis, Althusserian Marxism) applied to film which operate as doctrines and produce predetermined analytical outcomes. For them, a "Cognitivist" approach starts with building a body of evidence and seeks to test prevailing theories without them regulating the outcome.

In media studies, work such as that of Chin-Chuan Lee (1979) broke down the "grand theory" of media imperialism, arguing that the presumption that media power and influence follows economic power is not borne out on a case-by-case basis. In a similar vein, Michael Curtin (2003) has developed his "media capital" concept to sit between the totalising explanatory schema often seen in political economy of media and traditional area studies approaches which repetitively iterate empirical examples of country-specific trends in international media.

We also attempt to calibrate our cultural politics as a sort of "middle way" between revolutionary rhetoric and instrumentalist technocracy. Of course, any decent cinephile knows that Alexander Kluge warned that "the middle of the road is a very dead end" (*In Gefahr und größter Not bringt der Mittelweg den Tod* 1974, West Germany). But in asking what is at stake in the challenges to time-honoured hegemony in entertainment that this book traces, we draw more from American elite theory than from European neo-Marxist theories for our theoretical support. (The former posits that change can be driven by struggles *between* elites rather than the assumption, seen in the latter theories, that elites reinforce each other's power and influence.) Like middle-range theory, which attempts to steer between the Scylla of grand theory and Charybdis of boring empiricism, elite theory, while it emanates from the pluralistic side of the media and communications theory divide, affirms that power is structured in dominance, but that power centres are not guaranteed and can change over time.

This perspective correlates with Lash and Urry's (1987) notion of "disorganised capitalism", and with Robert Reich's (2007) claim that

DOI: 10.1057/9781137326454

large corporations have significantly less power now than three decades ago – and at least some of this can be put down to the degree of empowerment available through Web 2.0 and digital platforms. It also correlates strongly with Schumpeter's (1934) famous concept of "creative destruction" as a way of understanding the ceaseless volatility of capitalism and the opportunities for entrepreneurial agency it opens even as it destroys old orders. Hopefully without falling into the trap of over- or under-reading change, we focus in Chapter 6 on what progressive opportunities the new Kong Kongs of distribution might be presenting when compared to the old order.

Progress in making sense of it all

Ours is centrally a study of new players in the video, film, and television space where TV is at its closest to being reinvented within an online, broadband-enabled, transnational if not global, paradigm. It is important that we note the caveats and boundaries we have placed around the object of study of this short book. Of course, to even think of speaking of global reach is to speak supremely prematurely. In 2011, the population of the world reached 7 billion, but the number of people with access to the Internet reached only 2 billion. For most people, the digital revolution hasn't even started yet. Further, we readily acknowledge that mainstream television continues strongly, and in many countries is expanding robustly. Similarly, cinema distribution through the majors continues to be a highly profitable enterprise, albeit with a declining attendance base in the home market, with this being offset against revenue and attendance strength in rest of the world (ROW) markets and increasing ticket prices. The new "King Kongs" of distribution are a varied bunch: we speak of them as emergent global TV networks although this is more true of some than others. Most, however, are global in ambition and are in-principle transnational in ways that regulated broadcast and cable television are not and could never be.

What do we mean by the "reinvention" of television? We are beginning to look at television through the looking glass, as it were – at its obverse but increasingly familiar doppelganger. As we will see in Chapter 6, there is very little that is avant-gardist, postmodern or self reflexive about the new kinds of content platformed by the new players. It can look exactly like the most mundane of traditional TV fare. It can also

DOI: 10.1057/9781137326454

be very retro: second comings for B-listers and the resurrection of US daytime soap operas like *All My Children* and *One Life to Live*. But it also can be cutting-edge – for example, Netflix's adaptation of the BBC mini-series *House of Cards*, starring Kevin Spacey, with its first two episodes directed by Hollywood A-lister David Fincher (*The Social Network*), and an innovative distribution strategy which sees all 13 episodes of the first series released for streaming at the same time exclusively online. But basically, many of the new players are experimenting with a wide range of original content, a level of "off-Broadway" professional, pro-am and tyro experimentation not seen before in the mainstream TV space.

Of course, the transmutation of content is not the only analytical frame. There is a range of foci in the small but growing literature on online screen distribution. It can be classified broadly into: interest in the way current TV organisations, practices and routines are meeting the digital challenge; technical and regulatory concerns (a particular focus on the *International Journal of Digital Television*); and, on the consumer and demand side, contributions from the marketing disciplines and also analysts of user empowerment and potential democratisation of access. We review some of the key positions here.

It is to be expected that the main focus is on the TV industry as it is currently constituted. Thus, challenges faced by incumbency rather than strategies of the major corporate newcomers are the focus. Indeed, according to Perren and Petruska (2012), most of the "limited number of scholarly studies of Hollywood digital-distribution strategies thus far ... have tended to focus predominantly on the continuities in business strategies and corporate practices across conglomerates" (106). They attribute this in part to scholarly overemphasis on production over distribution. It tends, however, to play down the "widespread sense of chaos and confusion" (106) within the citadels of media power. Perren's work (2010; and with Petruska 2012) has focused on diametrically opposed corporate strategies (Disney and ABC's amity with Apple versus Time Warner's and HBO's enmity; and, even within the same company, News Corp's distributing *Glee* far and wide, but stamping down on any *ultra vires* circulation – or even independent discussion – of *Wolverine*). This underlines the explanatory power of elite theory, creative destruction and "disorganised capitalism" at these vertiginous points of transition.

The major monograph, Amanda D. Lotz's (2007) *The Television Will Be Revolutionized*, and significant collections in the field such as *Television as Digital Media* (Bennett and Strange 2011), *Television Goes*

DOI: 10.1057/9781137326454

Digital (Gerbarg 2009), *It's Not TV: Watching HBO in the Post-Television Era* (Leverette et al. 2008) and *Relocating Television: Television in the Digital Context* (Gripsrud 2010) make major contributions to our understanding of a complex, very fast moving object of study. But they only incidentally bring to centre stage the strategies of the major corporate newcomers, and the most recent developments around original content, TV-like scheduling, and multichannel branding.

However, when a number of the newcomers are the central focus, the research can be quickly overrun by developments in the field. Barr (2011) argues that Netflix, Apple, Google, and Facebook are "all highly dependent for content on the established commercial television networks" (60.1), but this has changed and is changing rapidly.

Of course, there are powerful voices reasserting the resilience of the Hollywood majors in the face of the digital challenge. Eli Noam (2010) argues that the "industrial efficiency" of the majors will see them not only survive but thrive. He bases this fundamentally on an exposition of the post-Fordist production arrangements evolved in Hollywood over recent decades, and the central belief that, in a field of burgeoning content and limited time for consumption (remember the attention economy), quality – aka blockbuster production values and budgets – will always be king. What Noam doesn't take account of is the bracing fact that Hollywood has almost no ownership stake in most of the new players and platforms, and the historical evidence (canvassed in Chapter 3) that, at points of transition such as the early years of TV, audiences have been prepared to embrace quite different versions of quality when what is gained is convenience and innovation.

The question of the significance of content diversity and its relationship to platform innovation, as we can see from this brief overview, is central to any qualitative understanding of what is going on in online media today. Bald commitments to, for example, "YouTube chang[ing] everything" (Gannes 2009) contrast with Lobato's (2009) review of the "politics of digital distribution", doubting whether the democratising potential of online distribution and any real diversification of film culture will be fulfilled, and directing our attention instead to the fact that the vast majority of online film consumption continues to take place in the extralegal realm. Situated in the middle way, Amyar Jean Christian (2012a, 2012b) has produced a series of close, nuanced studies of indie platforms, with a focus on the necessity of distribution innovation to go with aspirational production.

DOI: 10.1057/9781137326454

We are attempting in this book to catch the tail of the tiger – to lay a workable analytical frame over the very rapidly changing shape of screen industries which has deep implications for time-honoured assumptions and businesses. In doing so, we seek to engage with central debates in academic disciplines which study the media. But we also seek to engage a general reader interested in how to sense shape and pattern in the strategies of some of the world's highest-profile companies. We have written *Screen Distribution and the New King Kongs of the Online World* in a style that, we hope, will find that reader as well as offer rich material for classroom discussion and scholarly debate.

DOI: 10.1057/9781137326454

1

Online Distribution: A Backbone History

Abstract: *Drawing on industry lifecycle theory – fragmentation–shakeout–maturity–decline – this chapter outlines three waves of market leaders in the online space for the distribution of film and television. The first pioneering wave (1997–2001) was dominated by firms that were small, under-capitalised and ahead of their time. An initial shakeout stage (2001–2006) occurred when the Hollywood Majors moved into the online distribution space. However, they failed to establish profitable business models. A second shakeout stage (2006–) coincided with Apple entering the movie distribution business, and the launch of YouTube. By 2012, the third wave leaders consolidating their market positions in the online distribution space for film and television were YouTube, Apple, Amazon, Netflix, Yahoo!, Facebook and Hulu.*

Keywords: film history; screen history; industry life-cycle theory; YouTube, Apple; Amazon; Netflix; Yahoo!; Facebook; Hulu

Cunningham, Stuart and Silver, Jon. *Screen Distribution and the New King Kongs of the Online World*. Basingstoke: Palgrave Macmillan, 2013. DOI: 10.1057/9781137326454.

Looked at from a global perspective firstly, there has been intense experimentation in online distribution seeking to establish viable VOD business models both by and in competition with the dominant major studio players. Hollywood has been driven to undertake expensive and mostly unsuccessful experiments by the hugely successful meeting of global demand for cinema and television programs through informal peer-to-peer platforms. The "burn rate" of venture capital and other investment in the online distribution space has been very high for well over a decade and affords a classic case study of the rapid fires of "creative destruction" in a volatile high-stakes transitionary moment, because few doubt that digital distribution will, eventually, come to dominate both formal exhibition and household consumption in the most broadband-intensive, lucrative territories. The lessons learned from this history, largely of failure, are of benefit to those who are attempting to level the playing field for international and independent content makers globally.

However, almost inevitably, there is a concentration of innovation, in both platforms and business models, in the dominant US hothouse. This means that the backbone history of online distribution must perforce concentrate on the US. The next chapter will explore rest of the world (ROW) developments. It also means that international and independent content creators have either needed to establish direct links with the emerging online distribution market leaders e.g. iTunes, Hulu, Netflix, Amazon (and its European subsidiary LoveFilm) or deal through content aggregators that supply indie product to those majors, or alternatively by self-distributing using open-access platforms, for example YouTube, CreateSpace (with its feeder channel into Amazon Instant Video) and IndieFlix, taking on the task of marketing and monetising their content. There are, of course, exceptions to this general situation. The two most important are: the radical shift very recently that sees major commissioning of content by the emerging market leaders in online distribution, and the one big territorial exception, China – as we will see in the next chapter.

All firms entering the online distribution space during its first decade were confronted with the harsh realities of trying to establish a sustainable business within the context of a volatile, complex and emerging technological environment of what was becoming almost a new industry whose trajectory was unknown. Although some of the barriers they faced have receded, many remain. In the pre-broadband era, the principal

DOI: 10.1057/9781137326454

factors undermining the first wave of online distribution websites were those common to the majority of commercial ventures in the web 1.0, dotcom era, with the additional challenge that many of their wares were eminently substitutable through extralegal means. Online audiences suffered lengthy download times due to copper wire telephone dial-up connections and primitive compression software for large video files. Large flat-panel computer monitors were not yet available, so the viewing experience on small monitors was poor, and there were only clunky methods of sending film content direct to television sets. There was also a lack of high-quality film entertainment legally available online – most were B-movies or older film or TV content in the public domain. Added to this mix was the rapid shift of emphasis of "ripped" film content to online and informal markets following the Napster-led P2P "creative destruction" of the music business and the fact that software was available to digitise content and upload DVDs and more recently high-definition 1020p quality Blu-rays. A great deal of film or video content could be accessed illegally, anonymously and freely, with just a few clicks of a mouse.

Industry lifecycle and three waves of market leaders

In classical business theory, an industry's lifecycle is typically mapped in four stages: Pioneering (fragmentation), Shakeout, Maturity, Decline (McGahan et al. 2004). During the pioneering stage, barriers to entry in the industry are low and it is composed of many small start-up firms, seeking to exploit perceived business opportunities. This stage is followed by a shakeout as barriers-to-entry begin to rise, making it more expensive and challenging for aspiring entrants. This stage occurs when large companies either enter or begin to grow within the initially fragmented industry and mergers and acquisitions become more common as aspiring market leaders pursue growth and fight for increased market share by establishing larger operations that can yield scale efficiencies and increased profitability. This precedes the industry's evolution into a mature stage, typically of long duration, when an oligopoly of companies dominates a market with critical mass and profitability is high and relatively stable. The fourth and final stage of industry lifecycle – decline – occurs when the industry and its major players fail to remain at the cutting edge of innovation and are directly challenged by new

DOI: 10.1057/9781137326454

innovations, new entrants and/or converging industries that can better satisfy the existing customers needs.

In the online distribution space, during the pioneering stage and the longer shakeout stage that has followed, three waves of firms can be identified as market leaders that sought to develop sustainable business models, which resulted, for the most part, in widespread failure and many casualties – firms large and small, some well-financed and others poorly capitalised, from the US and from the rest of the world. We will cover those from outside the US in the next chapter.

The pioneering stage and first wave of online market leaders: 1997–2001

In the early days of the commercialising Internet, before the dotcom bubble burst, when barriers to entry were low and the future trajectory of the of online video distribution industry was yet to be determined, many start-up companies entered the online video distribution space, most offering short-form video downloads and/or primitive video e-commerce platforms. The highest profile pioneers to emerge during this stage were American firms: I-Film, Atom Films, Intertainer, SightSound, CinemaNow and Pop.com but despite their first-mover advantage most suffered under Christensen's (1997) "innovator's dilemma", being ahead of their time in an embryonic market that was not yet ready. These companies pioneered models and strategies that would later find traction. Their fate is discussed in the next section of this chapter.

Table 1.1 lists the key milestones in the evolution of the online distribution of on-demand film and TV content via the Internet in the US market from 1997 to 2013.

TABLE 1.1   *US online distribution of screen content, 1997–2013*

Year	Milestone
1994	First-ever VOD trials (via cable) in New York offer Paramount and New Line movies PPV
1997	IFilm.com launched as online video hosting website offering short films & trailers Netflix offers an online movie rental service delivering DVDs to the home Zoei Films runs first online film festival Absolut Panuska online experimental animated short film festival

Continued

DOI: 10.1057/9781137326454

TABLE 1.1 *Continued*

Year	Milestone
1998	BitScreen provides online lab for experimental filmmakers from July 1998 Atom Films launched online with short films and animated films Disney launches web portal Go.com with content from ABC News, ESPN and Disney
1999	SightSound sells first movie on Internet as PPV (Darren Aronofsky's *Pi*, 1998) CincmaNow launches first commercial online movie download service MovieFlix launches movie download service
2000	SightSound presents the first made-for-the-Internet movie Quantum Project Steven Spielberg's Pop.com fails prior to launch
2001	Sundance Online Film Festival launches Intertainer launches national VOD movie service in US Movielink, a joint-venture between five Major studios, announces online VOD movie service
2002	CinemaNow becomes the first VOD website to offer major Hollywood studio content Five Hollywood studios launch Movielink, a VOD download service responding to the threat of piracy Disney launches MovieBeam – a VOD service delivering movies via a set-top box
2003	CinemaNow movie library becomes available online in Japan via ADSL FTTH, broadband and set-top boxes (via Nippon Telegraph and Telephone data) Ex-Disney chairman Michael Eisner founds VEOH.com
2004	CinemaNow becomes the first major VOD site to sell movies as download-to-own
2005	Disney agrees to license ABC and Disney Channel shows to iTunes for the first time – market testing the download-to-own business model IFilm acquired by MTV Networks Apple launches the iPod with video
2006	Apple iTunes begins offering movies and TV shows as downloads to rent or buy Amazon launches VOD service Amazon Unbox (merges it with Withoutabox) Apple iTunes releases low budget indie film *Purple Violets* 1st direct-to-VOD release Disney's ABC.com first to offer free network TV programming online as catch-up TV NBC offers seven-day catch-up TV for select programs as VOD download-to-own and ad free CBS offers catch-up TV service for select programs containing advertising Atom Films acquired by MTV networks Movielink is sold to Blockbuster for under $6.6 million Disney sells MovieBeam for $10 million Joost launched as free online TV service also offers movies

Continued

DOI: 10.1057/9781137326454

TABLE 1.1 *Continued*

Year	Milestone
	Yahoo! CEO Terry Semel and Lloyd Braun announce slate of original TV style content and journalism that will be "smash-hit, medium defining programming"
	Online DVD rental store Netflix introduces Watch Instantly streaming movies online
2007	Disney experiments with subscription business model offering some primetime shows online as SVOD on video-enabled Sprint smart phones
	NBC Universal withdrew its content from iTunes over a pricing dispute
	Yahoo! originals slate put on-hold as web traffic numbers fall in turbulent year for media
2008	Hulu established as a joint venture between NBC-Universal and Fox and within ten months becomes #6 online video website using an advertising supported free content model
	CinemaNow sold for only $3 million
	Screen Digest estimates Hulu's ad revenues for 2008 to be $45 million and estimates online TV ad revenues for only 2.2% of all US TV ad revenues
	Hollywood forces iTunes and Netflix to remove certain movies from offer online as those movies enter the release window for TV markets.
	November: iTunes sells 50,000 movie downloads per day worldwide
	November: YouTube adds old MGM movies to begin migration from short-form video to long-form content and also adds High Definition widescreen
	Viacom and Paramount joint venture with MGM and Lionsgate to launch EPIX, a multiplatform premium entertainment channel, VOD and online service
	Screen Digest estimates US movie download market in 2008 at $227 million. Apple iTunes with 87% share dominates the online retail sales market (download-to-own) and the online movie rental market with 53% share. iTunes total 2008 revenues from online sales and rentals were estimated at $160.5 million. Hulu 2008 revenues were calculated to be $76.6 million (10% movies: 90% TV programs)
	ABC, CBS, NBC, Fox all provide catch-up TV for many shows within 24 hours of broadcast
2009	Hulu grows exponentially becomes third most-watched Internet video destination
	Amazon VOD introduces HD movies and TV shows
	Disney acquires 27% stake in Hulu via its subsidiary ABC Networks
	Financial analysts concerns arise about the viability of Hulu's ad-supported model
	Three senior News Corp execs including Rupert Murdoch, plus Disney CEO Iger, all signal Hulu may move to some form of pay/subscription or a mix with ads
	Hulu's growth rate slows, by July number of viewers have dropped -5% compared to April
	Internet TV platform Joost fails – its CEO blames his company's failure on VOD economics – stating control of quality content is critical

Continued

DOI: 10.1057/9781137326454

TABLE 1.1   *Continued*

Year	Milestone
	Under instructions from one owner, Hulu switches-off content supply to Boxee
	YouTube has 87% awareness and 56% usage; iTunes has 49% awareness and 10% usage; Hulu has 41% awareness and 14% usage – IPSOS motion study
	Time-Warner announces TV Everywhere enabling Pay TV subscribers to access content on any platform 24/7 using IPTV VOD Internet TV
2010	Hulu launches a subscription service Hulu Plus for $10 per month and then reduces the price to $7.99 per month but projects total revenues in 2010 of $240 million (approximately 85% of which is television content)
	HBO launches HBO Go
	YouTube places ads on illegally uploaded films passing revenues to rights-holders
	The Auteurs, the popular indie VOD site, is re-branded as MUBI
	Netflix establishes a $7.99 monthly subscription for unlimited movie and TV streams
	Yahoo! recruits veteran TV producers and journalists to "produce TV style content" but the initiative quickly stalls
	iTunes streams movies in Canada, Australia, New Zealand, France, Germany & Japan
	Amazon Studios launches providing independent producers and writers with an online script and film upload service and a first-look deal with Warner Brothers
2011	Warner launches Christopher Nolan's *The Dark Knight* (2008) and *Inception* (2010) as iPad apps bypassing iTunes to offer rentals and DTO
	HBO Go app achieves 3 million program downloads in first three months
	Netflix licenses first original programming *House of Cards*. Invests in other originals
	YouTube becomes a content provider acquiring indie studio Next to facilitate creation of original programmes
	Facebook begins offering online movie rentals with Warner Brothers' *The Dark Knight* (2008)
	Hollywood's answer to rival iTunes launches – UltraViolet VOD service enables audiences to own, download and stream movie and TV content on any device and stored permanently in the Cloud
	Hulu's owners disagree over core business model and decide to sell. Four bids don't match the asking price, so Fox, NBC-Universal and Disney decide to keep Hulu
	YouTube invests $100 million to create 100 channels of original content and $200 million to market them and redesigns the YouTube website
	Hulu has half the AdLoad of TV but surveys show ads on Hulu are twice as effective. Hulu launches in Japan ad free with web originals
	Yahoo!Screen re-launches intent on becoming major online video destination. Yahoo! sets up studio in New York and announces large slate of original online content

Continued

DOI: 10.1057/9781137326454

TABLE 1.1   *Continued*

Year	Milestone
	Facing increased streaming competition from Hulu and Amazon Instant Video Netflix expands internationally into Canada and Japan, plans for Europe and Asia
	Apple's iCloud storage for iTunes launches
	SVOD revenue grows 10,000% from $4.6 million in 2010 to $454 million in 2011. Tipping point as total online movie business doubled to $992 m. Critical mass market exists online – boosts ad revenues, subscription VOD, rentals and EST
2012	Hulu invests $500 million for Original Programming
	YouTube has 800 million unique viewers per month
	GooglePlay launched to provide direct competition to Apple's iTunes and Amazon using Google's Android operating system. GooglePlay merges its Android market (apps) with Google Video, and Google Music into one online store featuring movies, books, music and apps. Premium Hollywood content available VOD
	Tom Hanks' *Electric City* to debut on Yahoo!Screen. Viewership on Yahoo! increases 20% in Jan–Feb 2012, and Yahoo! becomes more popular than Vevo
	iTunes expands into Asia offering movies, TV and music on demand
	YouTube announces $200 million investment to market Original channels at the first ever Digital Content NewFront
2013	Apple iCloud surpasses 250 million users
	Vimeo introduces monetisation tools though its pay-to-view service
	$100 million budget made-for-the-Internet TV series *House of Cards* premieres exclusively on Netflix with unique release strategy and quickly becomes Netflix most-watched program ever
	Netflix: A second exclusive Netflix original *Arrested Development* attracts an even larger audience, estimated to be three times larger than *House of Cards*
	Hulu: Despite 4 million subscribers, Hulu is again up for sale following CEO Jason Kilar's departure
	Thirty of YouTube's most popular channels convert to paid monthly subscription
	Amazon Studios premiers 14 original TV pilots on Amazon Instant Video

The shakeout part one, 2001–2006: Hollywood's failures

A second wave of online market leaders emerged at the start of the shakeout stage around 2001–2002, when Hollywood entered the online distribution and e-retailing space as a strategic response to the intensifying threat of video piracy and the "napsterization of films online" and with the aim of exploiting the opportunities presented by online distribution (Graham 2002).

DOI: 10.1057/9781137326454

Sony, Warner, Universal, Paramount and MGM announced a joint-venture – MovieFly (later re-branded Movielink for the actual launch), a virtual video rental store offering films for digital download for a 24-hour period at premium prices equal to rental price-points in bricks-and-mortar video stores. Following the MovieFly announcement, Fox and Disney publicised that they intended a similar co-venture called Movies. com, but it quickly attracted the attention of the US Justice Department on anti-trust grounds following the MovieFly announcement involving five other major studios in a similar joint-venture, so Movies.com was abandoned. Disney however went ahead alone with its MovieBeam service, a digital set top box providing Disney content via the Internet (IPTV) to televisions in the home. Despite media reports to the contrary, these ventures were not only a response to piracy framed as an attempt to protect their intellectual property. The studios were beginning to realise the longer-term commercial potential in online distribution and through Movielink and MovieBeam had hoped to cut out any intermediaries by selling or renting content direct to online audiences within this new distribution channel. In a 2003 gathering of the National Association of Broadcasters, then Disney Chairman Michael Eisner stated:

> We are a conflicted industry. Hollywood studios spend enormous sums of money encouraging people to see its films and TV shows and then spend more money devising ways to control and limit how people can see its films and TV shows. Disney is mindful of the perils of piracy, but we will not let the fear of piracy prevent us from fuelling the fundamental impulse to innovate and improve our products and how they are distributed. (quoted in Olsen and Hansen 2003)

By 2005, both Hollywood-owned sites Movielink and MovieBeam had failed to establish viable online business models that matched the commercial expectations of their studio-owners. Despite the availability of "premium" content and the heightened diffusion of broadband Internet within the US, a critical mass of online audiences for legally obtainable premium content was slow to develop, uninspired by the major studios' offerings online – particularly at price-points matching "bricks and mortar" video stores. Both Movielink and MovieBeam were sold in 2006, for $6.6 million and $10 million respectively – knockdown prices well below the level of investment made by the studios. (All figures in the book are given in $US.)

There were even attempts by Hollywood to use the BitTorrent platform – the bastion of film piracy – to attempt to develop a profitable business model. In2Movies was a joint online distribution venture in

DOI: 10.1057/9781137326454

Germany, Austria and Switzerland by Warner Brothers and Arbato Mobile (a division of Bertelsmann) that used legal delivery of Warner Brothers movies and TV programmes via a BitTorrent P2P network that was established in 2006 but it closed down in 2008 due to intensive competition in the German market (Screen Digest 2008).

So from 2001 to 2008, Hollywood's efforts online through Movielink, MovieBeam, In2Movies.com and some other minor experimentation failed to make any significant impact on the uptake of legal downloading services for on-demand movies online or to slow the rate of illegal downloading. When taken together with the failure of Steven Spielberg's earlier aborted Pop.com (discussed below), Hollywood's major players lost combined investments of well over $100 million in failed online distribution ventures (Eller and Miller 2000; Reisinger 2007; Robischon 2000; Sandoval 2007).

Undermining Hollywood's attempts to dominate online distribution were two key factors: firstly, that the core cinema-going audience, aged under 25, was both the heaviest Internet user group and the age group most likely to engage in informal downloading – students had easy access to broadband services in their college dorms; and secondly, that rapid upgrades to technological affordances (faster broadband and better compression software) benefited file sharing P2P sites more rapidly than legal online distribution and e-retail video businesses.

Hollywood had failed to find the right formulas for making sufficient money in the over-the-top online distribution space to justify its investment and ongoing costs. For the first time in the history of the movie business, the Majors *voluntarily* pulled back from tendencies to vertical integration (studio–distributor–exhibitor/e–retailer) by selling their two online distribution businesses that enabled them to directly push content to audiences without any cut going to a middleman. It is worth remembering that it had taken a two-decade-long anti-trust case by the US Justice Department and finally a US Supreme Court decision in 1948 to force the Hollywood majors to sell their theatre chains and then further Justice Department scrutiny to deter them from trying to acquire and control the embryonic television industry in the late 1940s and early 1950s (Wasko 1994).

During the early shakeout, the pioneering firms faded either because they failed to establish viable business models and folded or were taken over and absorbed by larger companies. Viacom's MTV Networks acquired both short-form video content sites IFilm (2005) and Atom

Films (2006). Sightsound.com had patented and operated the first online video distribution e-commerce platform on which it sold the Internet's first movie on-demand – Darren Aronofsky's *Pi* in 1999 – and had also premiered the first made-for-the-Internet feature film *Quantum Project* in 2000. It filed suit against Apple for patent infringement after iTunes launched and General Electric then took a 50% equity position in SightSound in 2003. Although no longer an active player in online movie distribution, G.E. continues to pursue Apple in the ongoing SightSound patent infringement lawsuit (Garrahan 2012).

CinemaNow launched the first commercial online movie download service in 1999; it was the first movie VOD service to legally offer downloadable Hollywood content and was also the first VOD site online to offer movies as a download-to-own. The company was sold for only $3 million in 2008 after which new owner Sonic Solutions entered into a strategic alliance with Blockbuster (which had acquired Movielink in 2009), and the two operations were merged before Sonic on-sold the CinemaNow trademark to BestBuy. Intertainer, which launched an online movie service in 2001, was another early VOD platform during the pioneering stage of the new industry. Comcast, Intel, Sony, NBC, Microsoft and Qwest all became investors in the company.

Steven Spielberg's Pop.com had planned to produce short films featuring A-list Hollywood talent and distribute them online but it folded prior to its launch despite burning $50 million in establishment costs. It failed because of the classic innovator's dilemma – it was ahead of the market. It is notable that FunnyorDie.com is one of a number of commercially successful online sites in 2013 that uses the same basic formula that Spielberg had envisaged for Pop.com. *Business Week* noted, on Pop.com's demise, "Too few folks are sufficiently wired to get superfast broadband connections to watch Hollywood's Internet fare, and therefore too few people are willing to pay anything for it" (Grover 2000).

The shakeout part two, 2006–: disruptive third wave market leaders

Coinciding approximately with the timing of Hollywood's exit from owning and operating online movie download businesses, Apple entered the online on-demand movie business. Leveraging its previous success with the popular iTunes music-on-demand service, from 2006 Apple

DOI: 10.1057/9781137326454

began to offer movies and TV on-demand and rapidly become the lead-ing online movie download site. The rise of Apple was a disruptive force in the on-demand movie and TV consumption space, and together with the launch of YouTube in 2005 it presaged the beginnings of a funda-mental shift in the dynamics of the online distribution market.

Major change loomed on three fronts. First, a third wave of potential market leaders that had radically different takes on business models for the online distribution of screen content began to take shape. Second, streaming video, which would lay the foundations for a maturing industry, was about to be introduced into the online distribution mix as an alternative method to downloading video files to store locally on computer hard drives. Thirdly, the Hollywood majors led by Disney, Warner Brothers, NBC-Universal and Fox were about to embark on some further experimentation in online digital distribution on several fronts – from new day-and-date strategies that compressed traditional release windows to a TV-focused online streaming business.

The emergence of major disruptors was more apparent by the end of 2008. Apple's iTunes rapidly became the dominant force in the video download sector after the Hollywood studios sold Movielink. Using a sales-based business model offering Hollywood movies and TV pro-grams as download-to-own or rent at lower prices than video stores. Screen Digest (2009) calculated that by 2008 iTunes was capturing 87% share of the US download-to-own movie sales and 53% share of the US online movie rental business, with total US market size estimated to be $227 million and it was selling 50,000 movie downloads per day worldwide (Screen Digest 2008). However global supply was restricted in those early days as iTunes was licensed only to sell or rent movies and TV content in eight countries – US, Canada, Australia, New Zealand, France, Germany, Britain and Japan. The future growth of iTunes hinged on increasing demand from its large and expanding customer base for its "ecosystem" of cool, iconic, web-enabled mobile devices: iPhones, iPad, iPod, iTouch together with its Apple TV, iMac and MacBook.

Amazon began to emerge as a player in the online distribution space with the introduction of Amazon VOD, a streaming service for both premium and pro–am content. Like iTunes, it used a sales-based busi-ness model offering rent/buy paid downloads for premium Hollywood film and TV content and independent fare. Amazon owned other film-related Internet companies that together, provided an alternative path-way for non-mainstream filmmakers to self-distribute online, directly

DOI: 10.1057/9781137326454

engage an online audience for their content and build their reputations in the process. These Amazon subsidiaries were: Create Space (a video self-publishing platform); Amazon VOD (later rebranded as Amazon Instant Video); Withoutabox (a film-maker/film festival matchmaking service); IMDB.com (the online film and TV database) and Box Office Mojo (one of the highest profile box office websites). These businesses manifested a quite different take on the best business models to use for independent online distribution. Amazon has a huge customer base, operates a sophisticated customer relationship management system and has the ability to push promotional offers to customer's email accounts that are tailored to the customers likes. Amazon is also a known and trusted online brand.

Netflix began operations in 1997 as an online video store where subscribers ordered DVDs that were sent by US mail with a postage paid envelop for returning the rental. In 2006, it began a planned transformation of the business by introducing the Watch Instantly streaming service, placing 10,000 digitised titles from its 90,000 title DVD library online as a free value-added service to its large base of DVD rental customers. Netflix was focused on preparing them for the digital transition online and eventual demise of the bricks–and-mortar video store when VOD would replace optical discs as the second window after cinema release. By 2010, a monthly subscription service for unlimited movie and TV streams cost $7.99, plus an extra $2 if customers still wanted unlimited DVDs delivered to their home as well as on-demand streaming.

YouTube operated an ad-supported business model providing free user-generated content (UGC) that propelled it to become the most popular video site on the Internet with a 40%+ market share. However, its revenues did not cover its escalating costs (the net-specific phenomenon of *diseconomies* of scale) and from 2006, its new parent company Google was increasing pressure on YouTube to professionalise content in order to attract sufficient advertising to turn it into a profitable venture, and also to avoid litigation from Hollywood for a plethora of ripped content on its site. In 2009, YouTube introduced high definition streaming with 16:9 aspect ratio and long-form content through a deal with MGM to introduce old movies for VOD (Reuters 2008) and concluded a licensing agreement with studios that had no equity stake in Hulu – Paramount, Warner, Sony and Lionsgate – for premium content and back catalogue full length movies (Parrack 2009a). In 2010, YouTube Video Store launched as a geo-blocked service for US

DOI: 10.1057/9781137326454

users only, offering film and TV downloads for rental. Potentially a major commercial player in the OTT distribution space, YouTube had taken the first steps in a strategy to transform its company, to offer its huge user base premium content and become the dominant player in the non-UGC space.

In 2006, ad-supported free VOD programming was introduced online on Disney's ABC.com network as well as on the Disney channel. CBS and NBC also began operating VOD services on their websites offering catch-up TV for many prime time shows for a seven-day period after broadcast. By 2008, catch-up TV was being offered online by all of the US networks – ABC, CBS, Fox, NBC and others followed e.g. HBO GO and Comcast's XFinity on-demand launched in 2010.

Despite selling Movielink and MovieBeam, Hollywood studios experimented with new digital distribution strategies. Disney had been the first major studio to agree to license its content to iTunes in 2005, which enabled it to evaluate the download-to-own model on Apple's platform. Within two years, Disney also tested a subscription VOD model by providing a small selection of its primetime TV shows from the ABC and Disney Channel to Sprint's smart-phone network subscribers. Warner Brothers tested new release trajectories in the OTT space: releasing *The Dark Knight* to VOD online and via cable TV simultaneously, two weeks prior to its release on DVD in South Korea (Noh 2008). Warner extended this strategy to Japan in July 2009 with the day-and-date VOD/DVD release of *The Curious Case of Benjamin Button* (Gray 2009). South Korea and Japan were likely chosen because of the high quality broadband available in those countries and the respective penetration rates. Viacom and Paramount joint-ventured with MGM and Lionsgate to launch EPIX – a multiplatform premium entertainment channel, VOD and online service in 2008. And then came Hulu.

Hulu, founded in 2008, offered ad-supported free catch up TV programming and some films. It was initially a joint venture between NBC-Universal and Fox and marked a second, TV-focused attempt, by major media companies to control the OTT online distribution space. Despite the major networks also operating catch-up TV services on their own branded websites, Hulu quickly emerged as the leading streaming service online due to the attraction of its one-stop shop providing free premium television content from multiple networks, refreshed each week and with less in-program advertising. Approximately 85% of its

DOI: 10.1057/9781137326454

streams were premium TV shows versus 15% for movies at the end of the distribution value chain on free-to-air television.

Hulu's rise was phenomenal. Whilst YouTube's share of the total US market was 41% of all video users online, within 18 months of launching, Hulu had surpassed established brands with a 2.4% US market share (comScore 2009), making it the second largest online video site ahead of Yahoo!, Fox, Nickelodeon, MSN, ABC.com, MTV, Turner Sports, EDN and CNN but still a long way behind YouTube (Nielsen 2009). In May 2009, Disney purchased a 27% stake in Hulu, becoming the third major studio partner in the venture. Hulu's meteoric early growth during 2008 (measured by an escalating numbers of streams month after month on the comscore.com rankings) hinted that its ad-supported free streaming model might offer the promise that the elusive answer to the question – how can online video content be successfully monetised? – might at last have been resolved by adapting the proven network television model to the Internet.

However, the bubble quickly burst, as a view emerged among financial analysts during 2009 that Hulu's business model may not be sustainable because ad revenues for online TV were around 60% lower than for the same program shown on network television (Richmond 2009): the classic "analogue dollars for digital cents" dilemma. Hulu's growth by third quarter 2009 had levelled off, and it was left with little choice but to consider a subscription service to complement its advertising revenue structure. By September, despite having 200 advertisers, 40 million viewers and 500 million video streams per month, Hulu's revenues were forecast to be $164 million with losses of $33 million (Walsh 2009). In 2010 it introduced Hulu Plus, a subscription service, but had to reduce the initial monthly fee from $9.99 to $7.99 after the public failed to respond to the initial price point. By end 2011 it had 1.5 million subscribers (Roettgers 2012a).

VOD suffers from diseconomies of scale – YouTube was also facing a $470 million loss in 2009, with user-generated content considered to be a financial albatross. YouTube's viewers watched 75 billion videos each year but the critical issue was that the most popular videos were also the most expensive to provide due to costs of required extra bandwidth, new servers to cope with the growth, and escalating electricity costs (Manjoo 2009). The vast majority of YouTube's fare was UGC and ads were sold on less than 10% of its videos, hence YouTube's ad-supported business model for non-professional content was deemed unsustainable by its new owner Google.

DOI: 10.1057/9781137326454

Other notable players in the online distribution space during the period 2006–2010 were: Fancast (owned by Comcast, which at the end of 2009 was about to merge with NBC-Universal and thereby become a co-owner of Hulu); Vuze (formerly Azureus and a bit torrent P2P site), Guba (Time Warner) and Crackle (owned by Sony). Among the many other companies attempting to stake out their place in the evolving online distribution space during this period were: MySpace, which introduced video for mobile phones (Schroeder 2008) but it would soon be replaced as the leading social networking site by the phenomenal rise of Facebook. Another popular mid-tier social networking site Bebo continued to enjoy significant success with its low budget, made-for-the-web teenage soap operas engaging its 40 million subscriber base and enabling producers to retain 100% of advertising revenues generated (Bulkley 2007; Murphy 2008). Sezmi introduced the first true all-in-one open platform DVR box capable of providing video content from any source (Hachman 2008). Sezmi also provided a P2P cloud-based IPTV delivery platform for content owners and a subscription TV service to 36 metropolitan markets in the US that was terminated in 2011. Sezmi was sold in 2012.

The burn rate: further independent casualties

A number of well-financed firms that attracted heavy user traffic still failed in the online distribution space: Vongo was a short-lived online film download rental service with a small premium content library that was backed by Liberty Media's Starz Entertainment. VEOH was an Internet TV service that also offered both movies-on-demand and user-generated content and had former Disney Chairman Michael Eisner on its board, but burned through $70 million before filing for bankruptcy in 2010 (Richmond 2010). VEOH's CEO Dmitry Shapiro stated that his company's business model was unsustainable – despite its delivering 240 million video streams per month to 28 million unique users – because it delivered monthly revenues only of $1 million (Rayburn 2010).

Another high profile failure was JOOST, a P2P TV platform that provided films and TV on demand and was self-financed by the founders of Skype from the proceeds of their $2.6 billion sale of Skype to eBay – they also raised a further $45 million investment from venture capital firms (Business Wire 2007). Despite JOOST attracting 3.5 million unique viewers, the outgoing CEO Mike Volpi attributed its failure to copyright owners:

> Most of the economics accrue to companies that own the content itself and for the intermediaries there aren't any, that I can think of, profitable business models out there. The challenge is that media companies have approached the sector with more of a self-publishing model, meaning that content comes from their websites, as opposed to through aggregators. (Andrews 2009)

Blockbuster, under new ownership after Viacom had sold it, had acquired Movielink and continued to operate it on a sales-based model offering Hollywood movies and TV shows online to rent or buy. The intention was that Movielink would replace the bricks-and-mortar chain as video stores had entered the final stage of their industry lifecycle. Faced with intensifying competition from VOD and DVD rental kiosks, video rental stores were closing down worldwide. However, the financially troubled Blockbuster simply left it too late to make a serious play into online distribution, and in the harsh global economic climate from 2008 onwards with the absence of a new injection of capital, it became another casualty, filing for chapter 11 bankruptcy in 2010.

The shakeout swept the entire online industry, not just the top end. We conducted a longitudinal study monitoring almost 400 websites in the online distribution space from 2008 to 2012. We tracked 12 of the most interesting VOD sites that we speculated might benefit indie filmmakers by helping them bypass blocked traditional channels enabling them to bring their content to an audience online. From 2009 to 2012, eight of those sites ceased trading (see Table 1.2).

By 2012, the third wave leaders consolidating their market positions in the online distribution space for film and television were YouTube, Apple, Amazon, Netflix, Hulu, Yahoo! and with logic dictating that Facebook might even consider its options. Fourteen years after the introduction of on-demand movies for sale via the Web in 1999, it remains a small market worth just under $1billion in 2011 (Gruenwedel 2012a). Table 1.3 compares the relatively small size of the legal market for online downloading and streaming of movies in the US to the North American box office. But notice the growth rate: take off occurred between 2009 and 2011 as a result of rapid growth in Netflix subscribers, the introduction of Hulu Plus and escalating growth in Amazon Instant Video.

DOI: 10.1057/9781137326454

TABLE 1.2   *Changes between 2009 and 2012 to on-demand sites*

Sites still online and operational in 2012

CreateSpace: Amazon-owned self-publishing platform for book authors, musicians and filmmakers providing tools enabling independent producers to distribute their content on a platform with an established monetization strategy. For filmmakers, CreateSpace offers DVD on-demand sales via Amazon.com and streaming rentals via Amazon Instant Video.

Jaman: World cinema on demand and was a pioneer in developing social engagement strategies for its subscriber base. Growth has been hindered by the global financial downturn further restricting necessary access to additional venture capital and by legacy distribution contracts that prevent Jaman from being able to license worldwide rights to many of the films in its US library. Discussed in Chapter 2.

EZTakes: Focused on indie releases but has since evolved into an online movie store.

Indieflix: Indie short films on demand community where filmmakers and audiences can interact.

Sites that have gone dark

B-Side: Was an energetic online indie content aggregator with supply deals to Amazon VOD, Netflix, Hulu and iTunes. It became a casualty of the global economic downturn when venture capital dried up. It entered feature film distribution but could no longer secure necessary funding to continue operating. Shut down.

Heretic Films: Online indie films on-demand, went dark but merged with B-side.

Undergroundfilm.com: As an online indie film community website. Shut down.

Caachi: Online P2P self-distribution platform. Shut down.

Dovetail.tv: Online indie distribution platform. Shut down.

iArthouse: World cinema on demand. Shut down.

Zoie Films: World's first online film festival. Shut down.

Babelgum: On demand ad supported P2P web and mobile video TV platform with a mix of professionally produced content and indie films, shorts and clips. The website is non-functional as at June 2013. Whether it will resume operations is unknown.

TABLE 1.3   *US online movie rentals/EST* and US box office, 2003–2011 compared*

Year	$ millions US/Canada online movie sales revenues	$ billions US/Canada theatrical box office revenues
2003	4.7	9.49
2005	32	8.99
2007	122	9.63
2009	292	10.6
2011	992	10.2

* EST = electronic sell through (download-to-own).

Sources: Screen Digest; MPA.

DOI: 10.1057/9781137326454

Conclusion

In this chapter, we have provided an account of the short but turbulent history of screen distribution online structured around the classical four-stage industry lifestyle theory, suggesting that we may be coming towards the end of the second, shakeout, stage. While providing this overall, or backbone, structure, we have delved into the detail as well in order, principally, to illustrate the degree to which incumbency has provided no guarantee of success. Indeed, to the contrary, we have briefly profiled the "third wave" market leaders to emphasise a major theme of the book: the new King Kongs of the online world are, almost without exception, new to screen distribution when considered against a backdrop of more than a century's history of film and television distribution. These profiles will be expanded in Chapters 4 and 5. But first we need to consider numerous initiatives in online distribution outside the US "hothouse", some promising breakthroughs in providing platforms for more diverse, independent content.

DOI: 10.1057/9781137326454

2
Online Distribution Globally

Abstract: *This chapter concerns itself with the degree to which we can consider developments in online distribution outside the US "hothouse" to be significant within a "middle range" theoretical framework and a "middle way" cultural politics. The chapter surveys significant attempts to service "world cinema" and independent tastes. While a number of non-US online distribution initiatives act as vehicles for the further platforming of mainstream Hollywood entertainment product, there has been an overall broadening and diversification of the range of production opportunity and of content available to both national and global viewers. A feature of the chapter is a detailed case study of China's online screen distribution dynamics.*

Keywords: global online screen distribution; Youku; Toudu; MUBI; Jaman; iPlayer

Cunningham, Stuart and Silver, Jon. *Screen Distribution and the New King Kongs of the Online World*. Basingstoke: Palgrave Macmillan, 2013. DOI: 10.1057/9781137326454.

DOI: 10.1057/9781137326454

This chapter concerns itself with the degree to which we can consider developments in online distribution outside the US hothouse to be significant within a "middle range" theoretical framework and a "middle way" cultural politics. This is very much a story of constrained but at times significant developments. A good number of rest of the world (ROW) online distribution initiatives act as vehicles for the further platforming of mainstream Hollywood entertainment product, but overall there has also been a broadening and diversification of the range of production opportunity and of content available to both national and global viewers.

Online distribution, it must be remembered, remains an emergent market, the annual value of which was estimated to be close to $290 million in the US market in 2009 and only around $88 million in Europe (Loeffler 2010). (Data on its size globally remain quite speculative.) Nevertheless, it plays a small but growing role in ongoing structural change in world cinema markets. For most of the 20th century – the "American century" – the US dominated the world economy and Hollywood dominated the world's cinema screens. It is a baleful truth that "the majority of European films still do not find their way into the cinemas outside of their home territories" (Cineuropa 2010), but this also holds true for most of the rest of the world, including American independent films, because Hollywood's well-resourced release strategies consistently roadblock screens available for films from the rest of the world. It is a lock-out, or it seems that way from the other side of the fence.

However, consistent with broad structural change in the world economy – the rise of China and India, the beginnings of the "Asian century" – during the 2000s, several major theatrical markets increased local share (see Table 2.1) while those major markets which have never been dominated by Hollywood have continued their strong growth. This is a picture of an audiovisual "patchwork quilt" (Tracey 1985) rather than what was once lamented as a "one-way street" (Nordenstreng and Varis 1974) and is one of the fundamental drivers of a progressive global cultural politics.

Coeval with the earliest US online pioneers, innovations in online distribution were emerging in Asia and Europe. The first non-American initiatives were Korea's Cinero, a VOD website launched in 1999, and Afilmcinado, a "sparsely stocked alternative" German site with "horribly slow downloads even with a broadband connection" (Stables 2000), which went live the following year. *Exploding Cinema* was an online short

TABLE 2.1   *Local film market shares, 2000–2011 (box-office/admissions as %)*

	2000	2001	2002	2003	2004	2005	2006	2007	2008	2009	2010	2011
France	28.9	39.0	34.0	34.8	38.4	36.8	44.7	36.6	45.4	36.8	35.7	40.9
Germany	12.5	16.2	11.9	17.5	23.8	17.1	25.8	18.9	26.2	27.4	16.8	21.8
UK	21.0	11.7	15.4	11.9	12.4	33.0	19.0	28.0	31.0	16.5	24.0	36.2
Italy	17.5	19.4	21.8	22.0	20.3	24.7	26.2	33.0	29.3	24.4	32.0	37.5
Spain	10.0	18.0	14.0	15.8	13.4	17.0	15.4	13.5	13.3	16.0	12.7	15.0
Japan	31.8	39.0	27.0	33.0	37.5	41.3	53.2	47.7	59.5	56.9	53.6	54.9
South Korea	–	–	45.2	49.7	54.2	55.0	64.2	50.8	42.1	48.8	46.5	52.0
China	–	–	–	–	55.0	60.0	55.0	45.9	39.0	56.6	56.3	53.6
India	–	–	–	–	–	92.5	86.0	76.5	90.5	92.0	89.0	89.0
Russia	–	–	–	–	12.0	27.7	23.3	26.3	25.5	23.9	14.5	15.8

Source: EAO World Market Trends Focus Reports 2001–2012.

film festival run by the Rotterdam International Film Festival in 2001. That same year, a group of 34 French producers formed a company to collaborate and develop an online VOD platform from which to distribute their movies – UniversCine. This was still part of early dotcom era e-commerce, where most consumers used Web 1.0 via copper telephone lines.

There are obviously innumerable cases regionally of online distribution initiatives worthy of note. Japan's five largest film studios joint-ventured in 2009 to launch Marumaru Eiga – a PPV channel for classic and contemporary Japanese films available via the Actvila VOD service (Gray 2009b). Japan's most popular video-sharing website Nico Nico Douga and Yahoo/Usen's GyaO distributed a mix of free movies, trailers and music in Japan. Maxdome was Germany's largest online video store with a 45,000 titles in its library.

An Arab video-on-demand platform Cinemoz enables online audiences to watch hundreds of features, documentaries and shorts from the Arab world legally and for free. Its regional competition is Saudi television group MBC's catch-up platform shahid.net that offers the largest online library of Arabic feature films in the world.

As the major US providers such as Netflix, Hulu and Amazon, sought to move into Central and South America in recent years, a number of local initiatives responded. Most included premium content from Hollywood, but not all. High profile sites that launched between 2010 and 2013 with regional expansion ambitions in South and Central America included: NetMovies – a Brazillian Netflix clone; Uruguayan-owned Totalmovies.

DOI: 10.1057/9781137326454

com that launched across in 40 Latin American countries; Bazuca – a Chilean online video service offered Hollywood and locally made films; Terra TV Video stores, which operate in Brazil, Columbia, Chile, Mexico, Peru and Argentina with Hollywood and Latin American content; and Ideas Enteretenimiento – a Mexican online distribution platform that expanded into Argentina and Uruguay with plans for further expansion into Chile.

Smaller boutique sites include Yuzu (Mexico); Vesvi (Argentina); Vicoo (Argentina); Vemas.TV (Chile); Supercine.TV, an online distribution platform in Argentina with a small library of films including Hollywood content and independent, art and cult films. Peliplay is another Chilean entrant broadcasting content under a Creative Commons license to help online audiences discover new and emerging filmmakers. CDA offers free content from the Argentine Universal AudioVisual Bank plus documentaries, short films and series. Another Argentine Government supported online distribution platform was Conectate.gob.ar – an educational streaming portal offering movies, series and micros. Pixdom. TV, another Argentine service, provides a small library of 50 European and independent films.

And there are innovative distribution-cum-exhibition initiatives in the online distribution space. RAIN is a network of Brazilian digital cinemas that beams its films by satellite to 453 digital cinemas. It has exhibition alliances in the UK and India and also operates 26 art house digital cinemas in the United States. RAIN implemented a TOD business model that lists its film inventory online, allowing moviegoers, grouped together in online YouRAIN Internet film clubs, to recommend what films play when and where over its digital cinema network.

Table 2.2 is a digest of the milestones in the short but eventful journey in ROW online distribution.

We will approach online distribution globally, however, through highly select profiles in the key regions of Europe and Asia, where most online distribution initiatives are occurring. Then we profile the two main online distributors of ROW and independent screen content, Jaman and MUBI.

Europe

To appreciate the barriers to development faced by independent online movie services in Europe, one must add the powerful mix of public

DOI: 10.1057/9781137326454

TABLE 2.2   *Timeline: online distribution of ROW screen content*

Year	Milestone
1999	Korea: Cinero launches a VOD site
2000	Germany: Afilmcinado offers local indie films online
	China: e-Donkey P2P file sharing site enters China facilitating online piracy
2001	France: 34 producers collaborate to form UniverseCine VOD for independent films
	Netherlands: Rotterdam International Film Festival launches online short film festival Exploding Cinema
	Korea: Cinero offers films in high definition
2002	Sweden: SF Anytime VOD film service launches and expands into Scandinavia
	Netherlands: P2P platform Kazaa legally distributes Bollywood film *Supari* (Padam Kumar, India, 2002) online as a US$2.99 rental
2003	China: BitTorrent China (BT China) launches online with overseas films and TV
	UK: LoveFilm goes online
	Germany: Videoload goes online as Deutche Telekom's VOD division
2004	Italy: Rosso Alice offers films as VOD
2005	China: Todou, Joy and 56 sites launched
	India: Eros studio launches online store
	France: Five film VOD platforms launch: 24/24, CanalPlay, M6 Video, TF1 and TPS
	Denmark: Movieurope (FIDD – Filmmakers Independent Digital Distribution) founded
2006	UK: BBC iPlayer catch-up service launched, gains rapid popularity
	Australia: BigPondMovies launches VOD service
	Italy: FilmisNow launches VOD service
	France: Glowria launches VOD service
	Germany: Maxdome launches VOD service
	Sweden: Stockholm Film Festival goes Online
	China: Quacor becomes the first legal film download site in China; it offers free movies
	India: NRI site Saavn launches in New York offering Bollywood movies online
	India: Rajshri film studio launches movies-on-demand
	US: Joost launched as free online TV service also offers movies
2007	Spain: Filmotech offers "the best of Spanish cinema" online as DTO and VOD
2008	US: The Auteurs boutique independent cinema VOD site launches
	UK: BBC iPlayer achieves 250 million videos accessed online during first year compared to ITV's 80 million
	China: Voole becomes China's fourth licensed VOD provider (joining joy, 51tv and netandtv) Chinese government shuts down all other VOD sites
	Abu Dhabi: Getmo, the first Middle Eastern start-up offering movies and music downloads, fails to take-off

Continued

DOI: 10.1057/9781137326454

TABLE 2.2 *Continued*

Year	Milestone
	China: Voole makes a deal to distribute Hollywood studio content in China
	India: Reliance establishes BigFlix Online
	Korea: Cine21i reaches agreement with 17 Korean Webhard (online data storage) sites to identify illegal films in their catalogues and seek payment from users at the point of consumption and provide a revenue sharing service between Webhards and legitimate content owners
2009	US: Internet TV platform Joost fails with its CEO blaming the company's failure on VOD economics, stating control of quality content is critical
	Latin America: Internet portal TerraTV launches VOD platform offering entertainment, news and sports and makes programs available via smart devices and social networks
	Japan: Five Major studios (Toho, Toei, Shochiku, Nikkatsu and Kadokawa) form a joint venture to launch MaruMaru Eiga – a PPV movie channel screening classic Japanese films over the acTVila VOD service
	China: Joy and 80 copyright owners sue Tudou for copyright infringement
	China: Government closes 162 unlicensed online video sites
	Europe: 29 standalone online movie services close down in 2009 (Screen Digest 2009)
2010	US: The Auteurs is re-branded as MUBI
	US: iTunes now offers movies Canada, Australia, New Zealand, France, Germany & Japan
	US: Amazon Studios launches providing independent producers and writers with an online script and film upload service and a first-look deal with Warner Brothers
	Brazil: TerraTV video store launched offering movies for purchase, rental or subscription
	Brazil: Netflix enters Brazil to be followed by expansion into 43 central and South American and Caribbean countries during 2011
	Chile: Bazuca.com's OTT movies on demand service offers Chilean and Hollywood content
	AfricaFilms launches the first legal movie download site on the continent
	China: Youku launches premium subscription service streaming Warner Brothers' movie *Inception* (Christopher Nolan, US, 2010) for US$0.75 (RMB 5)
	China: Tudou licensed Warner Brothers' movie *Twilight* (Catherine Hardwicke, US, 2008) to stream on its platform
	India: Reliance expands cross-platform VOD offerings on online distribution, IPTV, DTHT with new acquisition DigiCable
	India: Eros plans to create a Hulu-style global streaming platform for Bollywood movies
	Russia: Ivi.ru – Russia's Hulu launches offering VOD movies & TV

Continued

DOI: 10.1057/9781137326454

TABLE 2.2   *Continued*

Year	Milestone
2011	US: Warner Brothers launches *The Dark Knight* (Christopher Nolan, US, 2008) and *Inception* (Christopher Nolan, US, 2010) as iPad apps bypassing iTunes to offer rentals and DTO
	Latin America: iTunes expands into 16 countries offering movies, TV and music on-demand
	UK: Amazon acquires Lovefilm
	South America: TerraTV video store expands into Columbia and Chile
	Uruguay: Totalmovies.com launches first legal premium online video content streaming service. Rapidly expands across 40 Latin American countries
	Argentina: Bazuca.com begins expanding its OTT movies on-demand service across Latin America, first into Argentina offering Hollywood, Chilean and Argentine content
	Latin America: 15 OTT providers offering on-demand content operate regionally as growth in Central and South American markets escalates
	Europe: GoogleTV expands into Europe
	China: iQiYi announces Y100 million invested to create original web content
	Shahid.net, first free Arabic VOD site offers series, documentaries, cartoons and other Arabic content. Shaid has world's largest Arabic film library and offers catch up TV service
2012	China: Youku and Tudou announce merger. Baidu buys iQiYi and invests $100 million
	Australia: Cinema chain and DVD kiosk operator Hoyts announces Hoyts Stream an online VOD service to launch in 2013
	Asia: iTunes expands into Asia offering movies, TV and music on demand
	Latin America: TerraTV rebranded as Sunday TV operates in six South American countries and releases Brazilian web series Desconectados exclusively online and commits to more original programming
	Arab VOD platform Cinemoz offers Arabic features, documentaries and shorts
2013	Movieurope website attracting less than 10 visitors per day and shuts down

service broadcasters, telecommunication players and uneven broadband penetration to the highly competitive environment that includes the dominant screen services of direct-to-home-satellite, cable and emerging IPTV services. To this must also be added the fact that video piracy has migrated online and Europe is the home of public, principled piracy advocacy. There are a number of online distribution sites in Europe's largest VOD markets, such as LoveFilm (UK and Germany), Glowria (France – films delivered online via Netbox), MaxDome (Germany) and

DOI: 10.1057/9781137326454

FilmisNow (Italy), that do show local films, and some have quite large catalogues. To survive commercially, however, and to attract a critical mass of customers and then hold them, their catalogues are mostly dominated by mainstream Hollywood box-office driven hits.

In the formal markets of Europe, online distribution is, at this stage, a peripheral supplement and has been greatly affected by the global financial crisis. However, despite 29 standalone transactional online movie services in Europe closing their doors during 2009, *Screen Digest* still reported overall growth in transactional online movie spending in Western Europe (rental and download-to-own) totalling €64.9 million ($88.46 million), up +85% from 2008, but equating to less than half the size of the US market of €209 million ($284 million), with 81% of all European online movie spending occurred in France, Germany and the UK (Loeffler 2010).

In Western Europe, satellite platforms preceded the diffusion of cable and attract the majority of high-spending customers who want Pay TV and a VOD service, whilst in low income Eastern European markets, where satellite and cable services are less predominant, IPTV via set-top boxes lead VOD development (Broughton 2009).

Despite Europe being a potentially lucrative site for the consumption of diverse film content, online distribution has not thus far been a lucrative market. This is partly because of the high up-front distribution guarantees that the major Hollywood studios demand for their product, and partly because large media device manufacturers such as Apple, Sony and Microsoft, and even larger online video libraries like Netflix in the US, used digital downloads like a retailer's loss-leader: selling them at below cost download prices or using them as a free value-add to the core business (e.g. Netflix's "watch instantly" was initially provided free for its DVD-by-mail subscribers). The only growth in the online distribution market came from the largest firms, which enabled the major studios to command higher prices for their movie packages. In these market conditions, the industry shakeout intensified because smaller, standalone online distribution websites did not have sufficient financial resources to sustain an on-going business and most will not survive if this scenario continues and venture capital finance to the sector continues to be elusive in the wake of the major financial crisis of 2008 and subsequent economic downturn across Europe and North America.

One of the most interesting European innovators for independent films, both from a filmmaker's and an audience's perspective, was

DOI: 10.1057/9781137326454

UniversCine.com, a VOD platform initiated in France in 2001, during the earliest pioneering years of the new industry. It was a collaborative vision founded by a group of 34 independent producers who wanted to develop an online platform that would eventually enable them to control the VOD exploitation of their films. UniversCine's goal was "to transmit and broadcast cinematographic culture, experiment with new means of distribution and consumption of films, and examine content, audiences and the means of renewing the relationship between the public and independent cinema" (Leffler 2007).

In 2011, about 50 producer-shareholders, who together represent nearly 40% of films produced in France each year and nearly 20% of films released in theatres, own UniversCine. The company seeks to "establish an open model, unifying and collaborative operation of independent films on VOD to become a leading player in this sector" (Leffler 2007). The website launched in 2007 with 250 independently produced films available at a rental fee of €4.99 for 48 hours of unlimited viewing (Leffler 2007). As a content aggregator and distributor it amassed a library of over 1,400 titles, mostly European independent films. French content now equates to about 40% of the catalogue.

A European Audiovisual Observatory (EAO) survey showed that in June 2009, UniversCine had become one of the eight largest French suppliers of content alongside major players CanalPlay, Virgin Mega, Club Video (SFR), Orange, TF1 Vision and two smaller players, Arte VOD and France Televisions (Lange 2009). In November 2012 Universcine. com offered over 2239 films in VOD and operated websites in France and Belgium. The longer-term plan is to evolve into a pan-European federation with new locally managed VOD platforms in Switzerland, Ireland, Spain, Germany and Finland.

A second European innovator in online distribution, founded in Denmark, was FIDD (Filmmakers' Independent Digital Distribution) or Movieurope.com, another collaboration-based distribution company that eliminated the middleman and sought to optimise the earning potential of independent films through its VOD portal. Founded in 2005, FIDD was 50% owned by "hardcore capitalist investors" and 50% by United FIDD (160 plus European filmmakers from 17 EU nations, comprising 40 Danish and 30 Swedish companies, 15–20 Norwegian, Finnish and Icelandic film producers, and various other European players). Involvement with FIDD was open access, joining cost nothing, and the deal was non-exclusive, so the producer was not prohibited from placing their film elsewhere on the

DOI: 10.1057/9781137326454

Web. FIDD's financing drew from three key sources – investors, revenues from VOD subscriptions and from the European Commission's MEDIA programme (Cineuropa 2010).

FIDD chose the subscription VOD pricing model in preference to a pay-as-you go rental or download-to-own fee because, as Jensen explained, typically charging fees of €3–5 per movie stream or download tended to encourage people to focus on mainstream films and choose blockbusters, because they knew the brand, while FIDD felt that it was difficult to value documentaries or short films in a VOD model. Consequently it opted for a subscription model and segmented the market, offering different price points for different packages containing varying quantities of films available on a monthly basis and themed either by genre (thriller, comedy, drama, romance, horror, kids, shorts, docs, fitness, erotica, etc.) or by the quantity of available films (platinum, gold, silver, bronze).

Movieurope engaged marketing partners who targeted their own customer base and received 20% of the revenues generated. CEO Niels Jensen stated no costs were deducted from the selling price and that it was a more cost-effective proposition to distribute non-mainstream films via VOD than to launch them theatrically. Movieurope had full economic transparency because revenues flowed back to producers based on an agreed formula that allocated points for each film in a producer's catalogue on the site – based on criteria such as admissions, budget, production year and duration – and then multiplied those points by the number of views. The extremely volatile nature of the emerging OTT market online was again emphasised when we learned that Movieurope had folded as this book went to press.

A European website particularly worthy of note for its cultural heritage role is Europa Film Treasures, which preserves "the treasures of our European cinematographic heritage" in an online archive and makes them available via a VOD site in five languages (English, French, Spanish, Italian and German)" (europafilmtreasures.eu/). A simple Choose–Discover–Watch click button menu allows users to stream European productions from the pioneering era of filmmaking through to the present day, which have been selected and curated from the prestigious collections of 186 films from 31 film archives from around Europe covering cinema from the late 19th century to the 1970s (europafilmtreasures.eu/).

The BBC extended its terrestrial broadcasting service online when it launched iPlayer in 2007 as a free, Flash-based, cross-platform streaming

DOI: 10.1057/9781137326454

service to provide a catch-up TV service to UK residents who can also download the iPlayer app onto a range of mobile devices to enable them to watch their favourite programs free when they are travelling or not able to watch them on television. It rapidly became a popular service and is now also available globally to non-UK residents as a free app for download on platforms such as iTunes, and programming is accessible if they pay a small monthly or annual subscription fee but they have only limited access to a much smaller library of content. The BBC also provides its programming with Britain's other major TV providers to YouView – another catch-up television service comprising freeview content via a broadband connection and a set top box. The BBC has also committed to Project Barcelona, which over time is a project to digitise its entire library and make all programs available to own for a modest fee. Whilst other nations and TV networks have launched similar operations to BBC's iPlayer, it stands as an exemplar of a public broadcaster that has very successfully employed a digital strategy online to promote and protect British culture and entertainment.

Asia

The region features the two most populous nations (China and India) as well as one of the most densely wired nations (South Korea) on earth. In the latter, pay TV reaches 95% of households, with cable, satellite and IPTV dominating the local market; so VOD via those platforms is well developed, even while the online distribution market is very small. Japan provides half of Asia's VOD revenues and has a range of robust domestic cable, satellite and IPTV services, so once again online distribution is still a small ancillary market. We will go into some detail on China as the most populous online nation and one for whom rapid growth in the shape of online distribution presages highly constrained but significant cultural change.

India has very low household broadband penetration but extremely high domestic cinema engagement. Informal market substitution effects are countered with market innovation, not state intervention. The distribution company Moser Baer, for example, drastically lowered unit prices of DVDs as a way of dealing with cheap pirated content and from 2007 this altered the DVD market (Baxter 2009). There is a plethora of pirate download sites via portals, social networking sites, film blogs and torrent

DOI: 10.1057/9781137326454

sites. There are also several legal sites, mostly belonging to the major studios: Rajshri.com, ErosEntertainment.com and BigFlix.com (which is part of the huge distribution concern Reliance). The key point about these sites, though, be they formal or informal, is that they are both accessed principally from outside India by non-resident Indians (NRIs) and by other South Asian expat communities desperate for the rich content that is largely unavailable in any other way. Most action around the online distribution of Indian cinema is from outside India, both from a consumption point of view and, indeed, in some ways from a distribution point of view (we will review MUBI and Jaman momentarily). This is another powerful overlay of the story of the globalisation of Indian cinema in general, and a useful synergy for Indian-based distributors for whom online distribution (that is, to overseas NRIs and others) and domestic release do not conflict.

China has the biggest broadband user-base in the world. One of the defining characteristics of Chinese film and video consumption is that much of this occurs online. By the end of 2012, China's official Internet population stood at 538 million, a demographic heavily dominated by youth and white-collar workers. Warner Brothers' research in China showed that 80% of Web users had watched video content during the past six months of 2008 (Landreth 2008), a statistic replicated worldwide (Rick 2009). There has traditionally been low domestic consumption of Chinese cinema in the pre-multiplex era of modernisation, and the informal market is huge – about 93% of movies sold in China are pirated (Cavernelis 2008). The informal online economy was, until recently, huge and dated from the turn of the century, when e-Donkey launched in 2000 as a peer-to-peer file-sharing forum. Followed by BitTorrent in 2003 and the two big YouTube imitators, Tudou in 2005 and Youku in 2006, there were at least 300 sites by 2008 – many illegal – offering video to a voracious public. In 2011, QiYi announced intent to invest CNY 200 million ($32 million) in development of "self-made" content ranging from micro-films, to dramatic series and variety programs (Businessweek 2011). Youku and Tudou merged in 2012 creating an on-demand behemoth and prompting a competitive response from China's largest search engine Baidu that acquired and re-branded iQiYi (AsiaMediaJournal 2012, Fingas 2012). A number of on-demand sites emerged in China but cater mostly to big studio mainstream films such as Voole.

Obviously, then, the online content market is competitive and volatility forces the state to take reform of the media seriously. For a nation

DOI: 10.1057/9781137326454

eager to promote its soft power, the potential is immense. As Michael Keane (2013) argues, liberating the potential of China's creative communities is a work-in-progress. While opening up media competition may be the best option for China to improve its performance and hence its image, the online world throws up unique challenges for the regime. In comparison with traditional, more easily regulated forms of print, TV programs and movies, online content distribution reaches across national boundaries.

Although the net population is large, only a small percentage is able to access YouTube, which like Facebook is blocked by the government. Chinese net users are encouraged to make use of approved online video sites; to date the most prominent of these are Tudou and Youku. Chinese Internet communities, particularly "grassroots communities", have willingly provided such sites with freshly generated content similar to the YouTube model. Community input into content creation as such represents a significant moment in the opening up the Chinese media-sphere. BitTorrent sites became available shortly after China joined the WTO. Because of the difficulty of distributing content outside of the official foreign film quota, which now stands at only 44 per annum, BitTorrent sites were a way for international content to reach the Chinese market; such content was often translated and subtitled by fan communities. In fact, most online video sites developed a mutual relationship with user communities and were prepared to flout copyright regulations.

However, assisted by a government intent on maintaining face internationally (or at least with the MPA [Motion Picture Association]), this mode of grassroots distribution was soon shut down. The introduction of the *Administrative Provisions on Internet Audio-Visual Program Services* in December 2007 resulted in a massive shake up of the audio-visual market, killing off BitTorrent-based online video sites or forcing them to acquire a license (Zhao and Keane forthcoming).

Upon the release of the *Provisions*, illegal consumption of downloaded film all of a sudden became difficult; incumbents jostled for alliances with state-approved enterprises such as Tudou, Youku, Tencent, Baidu, Shanda, Sohu and even traditional broadcasters like Hunan TV. Private companies sought out international content. In 2012, Youku entered an alliance with competitor Tudou. Because of the higher acquisition costs of US and UK content (movies, TV series), incumbents like the newly merged Youku–Tudou were drawn towards Korean and Taiwanese content, which was cheaper and widely popular among viewers.

DOI: 10.1057/9781137326454

As well as regional and international content, these new incumbents began to look to alternative strategies. In particular well-resourced industry players began to experiment. The most popular content genres are TV dramas, entertainment programs and movies. In-house production is an alternative to purchasing highly priced "Western" content although the term in-house generally refers to programming that is "self-produced" by the organisation; some organisations have even begun to assemble production teams.

The high cost of purchasing feature movies has resulted in so-called micro-movies, featuring content that is mostly culturally specific to East Asia; this is targeted at a fashion-conscious youth demographic. These micro-movies have led to more exposure opportunities for pan-Asian celebrities. The use of this talent pool has become a vehicle to tap into the broader Asian pop culture community. The upshot is that China has become a viable production centre, that is, production of content that can be rapidly circulated through the Chinese language world. Online, as development and pre-production doesn't follow the same protracted process of approval, involving significant censorship, by SARFT that is required in terrestrial broadcasting (for example TV serials), many new formats are quickly sponsored by regional investors. However, in 2012 SARFT decreed that all made for Internet dramas and micro-movies be pre-screened, putting the onus on the video websites to ensure that they were compliant.

The move towards producing original content is significant and demonstrates the attempts of the new content providers including online video sites and TV broadcasters (Tudou, Youku, Tencent, Baidu, Shanda, Sohu, Hunan TV), to differentiate themselves from the "national brand", that is, the widespread perception that Chinese audio-visual content is generally unattractive, politically focused, genre-limited and skewing old. Meanwhile the launch of CNTV (China Net TV) in 2009 signified that the central government is attempting to maintain a presence in the online world. CNTV claims to be China's largest online video repository of copyrighted content. Undoubtedly, this is true given its direct connection with CCTV archives but this connection doesn't necessarily translate into consumer loyalty. CNTV's stated mission to broadcast "China's history and culture" may likely be a recipe for consumer indifference.

The kinds of programming that are emerging on the dedicated online platforms (and the odd experimentally minded TV station like Hunan) are often experimental, using online communities as a kind of testing

DOI: 10.1057/9781137326454

ground. Youku began to develop so-called in-house production in 2008, before the price of TV dramas had risen. *Hip Hop Office Quartet [Xiha Sichongzou] Season 1(2008)*, its first initiative, was well received by online audiences. It continued to work on self-produced programs, launching Youku Originals in 2010, a brand of commissioned content that focused on everyday topics such as love and work. It is remarkable that Youku's Originals preceded similar moves to develop original programming for online audiences in the US by Yahoo!, YouTube and Hulu.

A notable development is the entry of TV broadcasters into this market place. Hunan Satellite TV, China's most adventurous provincial channel, licensed its successful TV series *Gossip Girl, Runaway Sweetheart (Luopao Tianxin)* to Sohu's online TV site to spin-off more stories. These two powerful organisations thereby entered into a cross-platform distribution and promotion alliance. Much of the talent for these programming ventures is drawn from Hunan's successful "idol" talent shows, *Supergirls* and *Superboys*. The strategy of Hunan TV Group is particularly interesting. Hunan boss Ouyang Changling has made it clear that it needs to look for new partners in the online video market and look towards the Asian market (Zhu 2012). Ouyang is critical of how the television market works in China, the waste of resources due to the proliferation of lookalike satellite TV channels (STVs), and the need to get approval for each program. As mentioned above, there is greater flexibility in the post-broadcasting world online, although this is constrained to entertainment genre innovation and not beyond.

In addition to drama series, micro-movies have featured in content production decisions, following the success of *Old Boys [Lao nanhai]* in late 2010. *Father [fuqin]*, the sequel to *Old Boys*, was launched by Youku in 2011 and repeated the original's success. Youku's next campaign was called "Beautiful 2012", and this introduced four well-known filmmakers, Ann Hui, Gu Changwei, Tsai Ming-Liang and Tae-Yong Kim, to Youku-funded micro-movies. Tsai's work *Walker* was selected to screen on the closing night of Critics Week at the 2012 Cannes Film Festival. Other micro-movies in the series were selected for screening at high profile international film festivals including the Shanghai International Film Festival, the Edinburgh International Film Festival and the Pusan International Film Festival (Youku 2012).

The success of these sites is no doubt due to the employment of popular Chinese and pan-Asian celebrities as well as "wannabe" celebrities. Youku's popular 20-minute talk show *Xiao Shuo [Morning Call]* (2012), is hosted

DOI: 10.1057/9781137326454

by the musician Gao Xiaosong who covers breaking news, from Oscars to the European Football Championship and even to brothel culture in China. The huge popularity of the program attracted the attention of Zhejiang Satellite TV. In September 2012, the program featured on Zhejiang Satellite TV. Other successful innovations include iQiyi's online celebrity interview program *Things About Youth [Qingchun naxie shi]* (May 2012), hosted by Zhu Dan, originally the number one entertainment program hostess at Zhejiang Satellite TV, and a talk show *Yide furen* (June 2012) by the well-known crosstalk comedian Guo Degang.

In addition to the celebrity-driven variety shows, the online space is populated by talent shows. Youku's weekly music contest reality show *Wo Shi Chuanqi [I am Legend]* began in May 2012 and has established cooperation with television networks and music companies (China Daily 2012). The contestants stand to win a contract with a television network or music companies. Meanwhile Sohu mounted its original talent show series called *Up Young [Xiangshang ba, Shaonian]* in February 2012, targeting the post-90s generation. The show is also broadcast on Hunan Satellite TV (HSTV), the first time that an online video platform and a TV station co-own a brand. Their joint efforts also cover content promotion and artist management. As previously mentioned Sohu's in-house productions often feature grassroots stars from reality shows produced by Hunan TV.

Chua Beng-Huat (2012) writes that China is a consumer of other's creative ideas and because of its political legacy is not capable of being a "sender" of its creative content to Asia. In other words, the "sinophone" (Taiwan, Hong Kong, even Korea) is where one finds the most interesting innovations in content. The point here is that China is unable to be creative because of its political legacy and a market place that is conditioned to historical recreations endorsed by regulators. The inception of CNTV bears out this point. However, the introduction of the *Provisions* legislation resulted in a rapid realignment of industry players. These new incumbents have united to look for ways to revitalise Chinese creative content, drawing on resources across East Asia and attracting new forms of investment. For example, Sohu, Tencent and iQIYI have teamed up to buy video rights under a video content cooperation agreement (Yu 2012).

In contrast to an image of China's media production as uncreative and heavily policed what we are seeing is the emergence of an East Asian market place in which China is more than just a low cost producer. The

DOI: 10.1057/9781137326454

fusion of East Asian culture together with programming innovations now flowing into China from international partners intent on securing a slice of the "world's biggest audience" (Curtin 2007) make this a mediasphere under construction, facilitated to a great extent by China's leading online video platforms. The question remains as to how the regulatory state will respond. In the past the state has contained its media by a combination of coercion and reward for performance. As the market gains confidence and finds its own way within the East Asian market, and as it draws investment and ideas from international partnership, the state, and its flagship operators of CCTV and CNTV will be pulled into this orbit of competition.

Jaman

Founded in 2007 by IT entrepreneur Gaurav Dhillon, and based in San Mateo, California, Jaman, with MUBI, is one of the two key independent online distribution ventures specialising in rest-of-world (ROW) content but based in the US. The company was setup for a total of $23 million from private and venture capital. Dhillon, a film buff, was surprised to learn that only 1% of movies produced each year actually gain a theatrical release (Scoble 2007). "Like a Sundance on the Web", Jaman allows the user to watch a film, review it, recommend it and see what the favourites were in Jaman's online community (Scoble 2007). The site is designed to facilitate viewing and discovery through trusted networks – seek, share and discuss with like-minded people. "We emphasised the international, independent nature of it because that is the least served. I figured I could do well by doing good" said Dhillon (Agence France Press 2007).

Since inception, Jaman has developed strategic alliances with prominent film festivals (Tribeca, San Francisco, Hong Kong, Palm Springs, etc), innovating in widening access to place-based culture. Until it became standard fare, a key aspect that made Jaman unique in the marketplace was the social experience it offered users. Jaman is sometimes referred to as "social cinema": a website which brings together the critique and review of a cinéphile website (the forums of Rue-morgue.com for fantasy film fans for example) with the social interaction, community and functionality of a social media site. Jaman could be considered a pioneer in this space, a leader in the packaging of commercial movie downloading in an interactive social experience.

DOI: 10.1057/9781137326454

Three quarters of all use is generated from outside the US; Jaman does very well in English speaking parts of the world, particularly current and former Commonwealth countries. The UK accounts for 29% of users, North America (US and Canada) 26% and India represents 23%. The consumption of Bollywood titles – one of India's mainstays – occurs mostly outside India, in the Middle East and the US BizShark's (Web) Traffic Heat Map showed that other countries with a small but growing Jaman user base include: South Korea, Japan, China, Malaysia, Egypt, Iran, Dubai, Pakistan, Finland, Sweden and Germany (BizShark 2011).

While Jaman had acquired 7,000 film titles by 2010 – one of the largest ROW online libraries anywhere – the actual availability across various jurisdictions is highly variable. Jaman has been unable to secure worldwide Internet rights to distribute the great majority of its films. So while Jaman's audience is quite global and the company's catalogue of licensed movies is impressive, many are geo-blocked and accessible only to viewers within the US. Moreover, legitimate VOD ventures such as Jaman currently compete against illegal BitTorrent websites and P2P downloading that do not have universal rights restrictions, and don't incur the costs of rights acquisition.

Jaman experienced great turmoil during the global downturn in 2008–2010 as venture capital dried up. To survive, Jaman has had to diversify into more stable business activity, particularly IT services, in an attempt to generate other revenue streams and to diversify risk. Founded in 2009, Jaman Networks is a "white-label" technology provider licensing Jaman's underlying technology platforms to companies looking to enter the online marketplace. In the words of Jaman Networks (2011), their service offers "content owners, retailers, ISPs and consumer electronics companies an end-to-end solution for worldwide Internet distribution of Hollywood movies, independent film and television content". While Jaman's growth has been inhibited by the unfavourable economic climate, it continues to be one of the most innovative online distribution companies servicing speciality independent and ROW cinema.

MUBI

MUBI is an online film streaming site specialising in important foreign, independent and classic film from around the world. Originally, MUBI offered two models for members to stream films. Users could

DOI: 10.1057/9781137326454

pay a monthly \$4.99 subscription fee to gain unlimited viewing access to a curated, rotating library of 30 films/month, with a new film option offered every day and expiring after a 30-day period. Alternatively, users could rent films from the MUBI library at a cost of \$3.95/film. However, MUBI revised its subscription package in 2013, still charging \$4.99 per month but restricting access to only one film per day, in place of the previous all-you-can-watch plan for the same cost. The push towards a more limited offering within the subscription package would seem to indicate that MUBI was having trouble making the economics of the unlimited offering work and the shift in emphasis is also indicative of how experimental business models are in online distribution. It is also notable that the new subscription package rolled out only in certain countries, underlining the general situation of markedly different content availability on the same platforms in different territories.

MUBI originally launched as The Auteurs in November 2008. It was the brainchild of Efe Cakarel, a Turkish born US citizen who gained a computer science degree from MIT and an MBA from Stanford. Disillusioned by the sites and services offering movies online Cakarel developed The Auteurs in order to "do it right" (Thompson 2010). To realise his vision, Cakarel furnished his business with a "combination of film geeks and AV nerds" (Zjawinski 2009). Partnerships with international distribution companies specialising in important independent, classic and contemporary films – Criterion (US), Celluloid Dreams (France), Costa Films (Argentina), Cineart (Belgium and Netherlands), Artificial Eye (UK), Bac Films (France), Hopscotch (Australia) and Martin Scorsese's World Cinema Foundation (Cineuropa 2011; MUBI 2012) – have enabled MUBI to build an extensive library that now totals in excess of 44,000 films. At the same time, software engineers "painstakingly tweak the compression settings for each film" in order to ensure users have a quality viewing experience, available for instant stream in any Flash-enabled browser (Zjawinski 2009), and through additional partnerships with Sony PS3 and Boxee (MUBI 2012). The company has plans to migrate their movie library to HTML5, which will further increase quality and allow MUBI to deliver its content on a wider range of devices including Apple's popular iOS tablets and phones. The third pillar of MUBI's platform leverages of social networks, enabling users to talk about films with other members and to check members profiles and see what else they like (Rawhiti-Forbes 2010).

DOI: 10.1057/9781137326454

MUBI faces a similar problem to Jaman, in that whilst it has built an impressive catalogue of licensed movies, licensing deals mean that many of the films are geo-blocked – available to viewers only within certain territories. However, while Jaman has signed significant distribution deals it has not been able to assemble worldwide rights to distribute films as effectively as MUBI, which has the advantage of strategically partnering with important global distributors.

The effectiveness of MUBI's strategy can be seen reflected in its global user base. Between its 2008 launch and 2010, MUBI grew to over 260,000 registered members across 177 countries. Recent figures suggest a significant membership growth curve, with registered members now exceeding one million (Butcher 2011). Of this global base, 55% of registered members where based outside the US (Thompson 2010). As of February 2013, the web metric service Alexa.com gives MUBI a global rank of 16,653 (Jaman, in comparison has a global rank of 72,588). MUBI is also popular in Portugal where it achieves a national rank of 1,971, in Denmark (2,498) and the Philippines (2,680). In terms of visitors by country, Alexa.com shows most visits from India (19.6%), followed by the US (17%), the UK (7.8%), Turkey (5.4%) and the Philippines (4.2%) (Alexa.com 2012).

The global focus is core to Cakarel's philosophy, and can be seen in the reasons for its 2010 change in nomenclature. Finding that many users remained unclear on the meaning of the word "Auteur" Cakarel approached advertising agency seeking to find an easy, memorable and recognisable name. Cakarel settled on MUBI – provided by a Tokyo agency – as being similar to the way "movie" is mispronounced in many cultures that have trouble with the letter V, and as the name of a town in Nigeria: a country recognised as a movie-industry powerhouse (Thompson 2010).

Conclusion

There has been as much initiative taken and experimentation in online distribution in major territories outside North America as we have seen, in Chapter 1, within the US hothouse. While we have emphasised in the current chapter platforms which provide access to alternative content than traditional Hollywood fare, it is also the case that much online distribution acts globally as simply another Hollywood release window.

DOI: 10.1057/9781137326454

And, while we have also focused on services which have survived to the present date (with one exception!), there have also been many failures in these early "fragmentation and shakeout" years of the establishment of screen distribution online. Consistent with broad structural change in the world economy, we have emphasised developments in India and China. The latter provides an intriguing case study of initially imitative strategy but then powerfully autochthonous content development. Now returning, in the next chapter, to the US engine of innovation, we frame the rapidly evolving present against a backdrop of major battles for control of the screen industry in the early- and mid-20th century.

DOI: 10.1057/9781137326454

3
Lessons from History, the Future of Television?

Abstract: *This chapter considers historical comparisons to the current period of digital disruption, discussing two periods in the history of Hollywood where powerful incumbent market leaders have been seriously challenged by new competitors. The first was from 1917 to 1927 during the "Theater Wars" when Hollywood's dominant studio-distributor was challenged by the emergence of vertically integrated studio–distributor–exhibitors. The second was from 1948 to 1958 when commercial television began to diffuse widely into American homes, fragmenting regular movie-going audiences. We argue that these comparisons hold strategic lessons for the present by focusing on the advantages that companies have that control the platforms that deliver content to audiences. As an introduction to the following chapters, this chapter introduces criteria for what makes a TV network.*

Keywords: US film history; future of television; television networks; patent wars; theater wars; Thomas Edison; Adolph Zukor; Carl Laemmle

Cunningham, Stuart and Silver, Jon. *Screen Distribution and the New King Kongs of the Online World.* Basingstoke: Palgrave Macmillan, 2013. DOI: 10.1057/9781137326454.

Similar to today's emerging battle for supremacy in online distribution, there were struggles to control the early screen industry – which, for the first half of the 20th century, meant only movies. Ramsaye (1986, 793) highlighted four battles for industry dominance during the silent era that may hold lessons for today's emerging players in online distribution.

The first was waged by Thomas Edison and was based on patent control. The second, also initiated by Edison, was to make peace with his rivals and together pool their patents for film equipment, in an attempt to monopolise the US market. The third, won by Adolph Zukor's Famous Players-Paramount, was a battle based on product innovation to win-over the mass audience from Edison's Trust and the old-line movie studios that had dominated the industry with a business model based on cheaper, lower quality short films. The fourth battle again involved Paramount, against a new rival – First National and was another battle for eyeballs – this time for distribution access to America's most profitable theatre screens and the mass audience. These struggles may hold potential lessons for today's players in online distribution and are discussed briefly below as "The Patent Wars" and "The Theater Wars".

It is arguable that the only other moment during which the incumbent leaders' market position was seriously undermined, again by innovation, occurred around 1948–1958 when commercial television began to diffuse widely into American homes. Hollywood's major studios lost the regular mass movie-going audience as many stayed home to watch TV and a steep decline in cinema attendance began, as a second period of creative destruction impacted the major studios and movie theatres and a second screen industry offering in-home moving picture entertainment proved a cheaper substitute.

The patent wars

The first battle over patent control was initiated by Thomas Edison, who had invented the first commercial moving picture camera (the kineto-graph), the first moving picture viewing-device (the kinetoscope, a coin-operated peep hole device found in amusement parlours) and whose company Edison Manufacturing built the world's first movie studio (the Black Maria in New Jersey).

Edison aggressively pursued competitors through patent infringement litigation from 1898 to 1908 (Puttnam 1998, 46–47) in an attempt to

DOI: 10.1057/9781137326454

undermine emerging competitors in the fledgling industry. Such lawsuits were central to his strategy to try to eliminate smaller, under-capitalised rivals that had infringed his patents and could not afford the legal costs, and was part of a longer-term strategy to wear down his larger, more powerful and well-financed rivals over time. A few years earlier in 1892, the Edison General Electric company employed exactly the same litigation strategy based on patent infringements to contain rivals and dominate the electric lamp industry (Reich 1992).

When Edison launched his patent wars in the film industry, it is unlikely that he anticipated an exhausting, ten-year battle for supremacy with the other pre-Hollywood major American studios – Biograph, Vitagraph, Lubin, Selig, Essanay and Kalem. He certainly did not antici-pate the emergence of a competitor with the size and scale and financial muscle of the massive French film conglomerate Pathe Freres or that European firms, led by Pathe, would enter the US market during the nickelodeon era and pose a more formidable threat than even his local American rivals. Edison's strategy to achieve dominance of the fledgling film industry based on patent control failed.

The cost of the patent wars severely weakened all parties and led to the second major struggle to control the industry when Edison persuaded his major American rivals and the world's largest film con-glomerate, Pathe Freres, to co-venture with him and form the Motion Picture Patents Company (MPPC). Also known as "The Trust", the MPPC did a deal with Kodak to secure exclusive use of its film stock. The MPPC pooled 17 patents – 1 for film, 2 for camera equipment and 14 for projectors – and was established to monopolise the American film market. The MPPC established the General Film Company in 1911 as the first national distribution operation within the American market and these two companies worked in-tandem, to try to force all production companies and exhibitors to use only MPPC cameras and projectors. This had serious implications for producers and exhibitors in America. Unlicensed producers would no longer be able to get their films exhibited in any MPPC-licensed theatres, thus blocking their access to thousands of screens across America from nickelodeons and store-front theatres to the emerging permanent movie theatres. And the reverse applied to unlicensed independent exhibitors who faced an immediate product shortage from the loss of supply of films from producers who were MPPC licensed because they used MPPC patented cameras.

DOI: 10.1057/9781137326454

Edison's second attempt to dominate the industry failed within six years because his licensing strategy failed to control the only distribution platform – cinema screens. The MPPC operated from 1909 to 1915 when it was ordered to dissolve under anti-trust legislation. However the reality was that market conditions had changed dramatically from 1909 when Carl Laemmle (who three years later founded Universal Studios) led an independent movement of producers and exhibitors against the MPPC that destroyed the latter's market power due to two disruptive innovations – the creation of the movie star system and the introduction of longer, bigger budget feature films by Adolph Zukor's Famous Players studio. The result was a rapid escalation of market demand for the independent movement's films as audiences became fascinated by movie stars and as higher quality, more complex movie narratives emerged and popular tastes became more sophisticated.

The MPPC was focused on mass production of low-cost short films featuring unbilled casts. Laemmle was an exhibitor and distributor who launched his own production company, IMP films, in 1909 in order to provide films for his own theatres using non-MPPC projectors. He saw the opportunity to differentiate IMP by adapting the live theatre's system giving lead players star billing to the moving picture industry and he launched the career of Florence Lawrence as the first billed movie star.

Adolph Zukor founded his studio Famous Players in 1912 and within five years he also acquired the national distribution company Paramount Pictures. Zukor introduced the first American-made feature-length movies into the US market and by 1917 Famous Players–Lasky–Paramount had become the largest Hollywood conglomerate. Its rapid growth was driven by a two-pronged strategy that contracted the most popular movie stars and produced a massive annual production output – enough to satisfy any movie theatre's annual demand for two new films per week.

Zukor won the third battle for supremacy in the industry because audiences wanted Paramount's star-powered movies and exhibitors paid premium prices to secure them.

The key difference between the MPPC approach that sought dominance based on patent protection and litigation and that of the emerging Hollywood studios led by Paramount was that the latters' operations were focused on a mass-market, quality-based business strategy leveraging movie stars, bigger budgets, longer films and more elaborate production values to differentiate them from the MPPC's low-cost short films.

DOI: 10.1057/9781137326454

During this same period the first permanent movie theatres were being constructed and embryonic cinema circuits were emerging.

The theatre wars

From around 1911, America's first movie theatre circuits began to emerge and by 1917, Famous Players–Paramount had grown rapidly to become the largest producer and distributor of feature films in the world (Hampton 1970, 174). It dominated the US market because the most popular movie stars were contracted to the studio enabling Paramount to charge movie theatres premium prices (for film rentals) and enforce block booking (they had to buy a package of films to get the most prestigious Paramount pictures featuring the biggest stars). A group of theatre owners who were unwilling to meet Paramount's increasingly high terms of business formed the First National Theatre circuit and then vertically integrated, forming their own film studio and distribution company – First National Pictures.

Despite its size and scale as a vertically integrated producer–distributor possessing the largest "stable" of the most popular movie stars on-contract, the largest annual production output of any Hollywood studio in the industry's history, an unrivalled national distribution powerhouse and profitability that was the envy of its competitors, Paramount was strategically exposed through the unanticipated formation of First National. Its new rival threatened to block its access to the most lucrative first-run movie theatre screens across the country by boycotting Paramount movies and replacing them with its own star-driven First National productions.

This move posed a significant competitive threat to the rest of the industry (Balio 1985, 450). Paramount and its President and owner Adolph Zukor responded by borrowing heavily to vertically integrate and rapidly develop a national cinema chain. There is no historical evidence to suggest that prior to the rise of First National that Zukor showed any intentions of acquiring theatre circuits. In his autobiography, he defends the acquisition – "our company began to buy theatres including strings of them"– as self-defence (Zukor 1953, 194–195).

For two years, Zukor had closely studied First National strategy and business practices from the inside after he had quietly acquired a number of First National theatre franchises. He then moved quickly with a well-planned and

DOI: 10.1057/9781137326454

well-financed program of national theatre expansion securing or building a sufficient number of first run houses in key markets across the country and overseas that would provide certainty that Famous Players films would play on the best screens and reach mass audiences (Puttnam 1998, 254). The theatre acquisition programs were funded by bank loans, but the cinema real estate provided collateral to the banks and other investors to guarantee cash flow enabling Paramount to secure further loans to finance the studios' annual production slates. This strategy underpinned the Hollywood majors' business model from the 1920s to 1950s.

As these Theatre Wars erupted, smaller rivals like Loews Theatres and Fox Film that operated regional circuits were forced into action and also had to develop a national circuit just to stay in the game (Huettig 1944, 37; Puttnam 1998, 259–260) and in an "aggressive race for theatre acquisition" (Lewis 1933, 22–23) hundreds of independent exhibitors were forced out (Balio 1985, 120). Zukor undermined First National when Paramount acquired its key franchise – the Balaban and Katz theatre circuit and it became the cornerstone of the Paramount Publix branded cinema chain run by Barney Balaban and Sam Katz. Warner Brothers acquired the rest of First National in 1928.

So by the advent of talking pictures in 1927, the Big Five (Paramount, Loews-MGM, Warner Brothers-First National, Fox and RKO) vertically integrated studios had consolidated and established themselves as "The Majors" that would dominate the movie business and Paramount and Loews-MGM were the world's largest and most powerful theatre owners (Puttnam 1998, 275). The "Little Three" (Universal, Columbia and UA) were producer–distributors but did not operate national theatre circuits.

Film production is inherently high-risk – no one can accurately predict which movies will work. Film distribution can be a more stable, profitable business because risk can be spread across a slate of pictures – some will win, some will lose and powerful distribution provides market power when negotiating with exhibitors. The reality was that the Majors really only consolidated their market power by controlling the platform (movie theatre screens) needed to reach the mass audience for movies at that point in history – vertical integration into exhibition and control of the most profitable first-run movie theatres underpinned their ability to dominate the industry until the 1948 when they were required to sell their theatre holdings by a US Supreme Court ruling.

Edison's litigation-driven attempts to control the industry through enforcing patents failed due to market-driven innovations that satisfied

DOI: 10.1057/9781137326454

changing audience tastes. In the same vein, Hollywood today has failed to stem video piracy despite employing litigation and an onslaught of other aggressive tactics in the face of changing audience demand and dynamics. The Theatre Wars demonstrate that even the most powerful studio-distributor in any era is ultimately reliant on broad-enough platforms to access audiences. Despite winning control of the industry with the best films, most of the biggest stars, and the best distribution, Zukor found that First National was suddenly blocking the most profitable screens. Tim Wu's *The Master Switch* (2010), which traces the "long cycle" of competitive information empires becoming oligopolistic, reopening only after disruptive innovation, comments on Laemmle and Zukor:

> Laemmle's bold decision, like Zukor's earlier, presents an interesting example of dynamics we have observed before. We have seen how important outsiders are to industrial innovation: they alone have the will or the interest to challenge the dominant industry.... Laemmle's instinctive loathing of the Trust's domination, his desire to be free, would have a deep and lasting effect on American film. (Wu 2010, 66)

We liken today's online landscape to the late 1910s and the period of the Theatre Wars.

TV – the second screen woos away the weekly cinema audience

The second historical scenario that may hold lessons for contemporary players in the emerging online space for online distribution picks up the story at that point in the 1950s when the Majors sold their theatre chains and television began to impact the movie market. Despite radio's effect on cinema attendances from 1920, and particularly during the Great Depression, it did not have the degree of potential substitutability that TV represented. The introduction of TV was only the second time in the industry's history that the dominant corporations faced a potentially fatal threat from a disruptive technology that could directly undermine the movie business. Oscar-winning independent producer and former President of Columbia Pictures – David Puttnam observed:

> What really troubled the studio bosses was that TV had developed outside their control. Since the early 1920s they had grown accustomed to the idea that they were the undisputed kings of the moving picture industry. ... Now a group of upstarts (NBC and CBS) had struck at the very roots of

DOI: 10.1057/9781137326454

their authority by creating moving pictures that could be fed directly into people's homes. (1998, 183)

During the 1950s, television replaced movie going as the most popular form of screen entertainment. It was introduced at a time when social and cultural dynamics were also shifting substantially. From the peak box office year of 1946, when returning servicemen joined wives and girlfriends at the movies and inflated cinema audiences, before settling down in suburbia and raising families, the post-war population boomed, the economy grew along with a burgeoning middle class affluence and adults began to abandon the pre-war habit of a weekly trip to the movies in favour of a technology that fitted such trends perfectly. In 1950, TV penetration into American households was 9%, by the end of the decade it was 86% and cinema admissions had dropped 45% over the same time period (Gomery 1985).

The composition of the regular movie-going audience changed. *Variety* (1959) reported results from a leading market research firm that found that the primary audience was less than 30 years old, and that frequency of attendance increased with education level. This is an almost complete reversal from the 1940s and earlier decades, when the family made a weekly trip as part of a regular movie-going habit to the local movie theatre. By the 1960s adults now seemed to prefer staying home to watch free programs on TV. On the other hand, young adults and teenagers with increased spending power and access to cars wanted to socialise out of home. Movies were an integral part of an emerging youth culture, with new values radically different from previous generations and shaped by a wave of turbulent social, cultural and political upheaval sweeping across America and the Western world. The profile of the core movie-going audience was now younger, better educated and more affluent.

Like the Theatre Wars scenario, the longer-term winners in television were the companies that controlled the new platform, the moving picture industry's second screen. Some of the Major studios – Paramount, Fox and Warner Brothers – had initially tried to gain control of the emergent TV Industry through strategic investments in early television stations and networks (Wasko 1994, 11–14). However as the Major studios were then under investigation by the Department of Justice for anti-trust violations (that would eventually lead to the 1948 Supreme Court decision forcing them to sell their theatre chains), a foray into the fledgling television industry was not viable (Kindem 1982; Puttnam 1998, 181).

DOI: 10.1057/9781137326454

Unable to control television, the Majors tried to kill it in its infancy by refusing to supply the TV networks with their movies for the first half of the decade. The emerging networks therefore had to commission their own content. The timing proved fortunate for the fledgling television industry because it coincided with the collapse of the old studio system, and as former studio-employed producers and technicians became independent contractors when the studios let them go, many migrated to television (Sklar 1994, 282).

TV production proved to be fertile ground for independent producers trying to establish themselves in Hollywood in the post-studio era. As small businesses with much lower overheads than the Majors, they could provide low budget programming to the new TV networks. For example, Lucille Ball and Desi Arnaz produced *I Love Lucy*, and by the mid fifties their company Desilu made more program hours than any of the major studios. As we saw in the Introduction, this is the kind of industrial efficiency that Eli Noam lauded.

Initially television production values were low because budgets were low and the new medium was experimental. The business model was based on radio with program sponsors providing revenues and audience tastes were relatively unsophisticated. So in the absence of Hollywood movies and Hollywood stars, the TV networks developed their own stars or poached talent from radio (Puttnam 1998, 183–184).

NBC, CBS and ABC established themselves as the dominant forces in the new medium and were unchallenged by serious rivals until the cable TV boom of the 1980s. Cinema attendance declined dramatically from 1948–1974 as audiences stayed home to watch free-to-air TV and the small screen defeated the big screen in the second great "battle for eyeballs". Once again, victory went to the corporations that controlled the platform able to reach the widest audience – broadcast TV.

By the mid-1950s, some Major Hollywood studios began selling movies to television and by the late 1950s most had also begun supplying TV shows to the networks. Puttnam (1998, 194) notes: "The American studios had largely made peace with television by the mid-1950s. The leaders of the American movie business had found a way of exploiting television that enabled them to start rebuilding their industry from the wreckage of the studio system".

TV posed a far more serious threat to the Majors than their "first screen" competitors. We analysed *Variety*'s end-of-year US box office charts from Hollywood's peak year in 1946 onwards until 1975 (a period during which black and white and then colour TV were introduced) and noted that in the two years in which the Major studios' combined share of the annual box office in the world's largest film market reached its lowest historical points – 1958 (the Majors 89%, the rest 11%) as TV diffused widely and 1971 (the Majors 78%, the rest 22%) as colour TVs also began to diffuse in the US market – the Majors experienced severe financial crisis.

Colour TV was introduced in 1967, cinema attendance declined further and many big budget studio movies also failed at the box office, and for the period 1969–1971 six of the eight studios reported financial losses in one of those three years and three studios reported financial losses in two of those years (Jowett and Linton 1980, 38). One by one the Majors were taken over by larger conglomerates. A critical point to note is that at the point of the Major studios' greatest vulnerability (or at any time in their steep decline from 1949–1974) there were no film studio or distribution rivals anywhere in the world that produced a pipeline with sufficient volume of films commercially attractive enough to exhibitors and audiences to displace the Hollywood movies on the world's cinema screens. It was an absence of a quality alternative product supply and their strength in global distribution that enabled the Hollywood majors to retain their market dominance, despite verging on bankruptcy.

Learning from history

Both historic scenarios hold strategic lessons for the creative destruction that we are witnessing in the movie, video, TV and cable industries today. They demonstrate that despite powerful market incumbency, the companies that control the platforms that deliver content to audiences can win the battle for audiences and that in both historical instances they needed to create their own content in the early days of the emerging industry. The 1950s TV scenario also suggests that early mass audiences will accept alternatives to established quality during periods of innovation. This emphasises that what counts as (widely accepted, premium) content can change during periods of major disruption, and that therefore the arguments which we have seen advanced in the Introduction by Eli Noam, for example, for "content is king" need to be historicised.

DOI: 10.1057/9781137326454

Future television networks?

Zooming forward from the beginnings of television to its possible future shape, the composition of an effective oligopoly likely to dominate the online television space is beginning to take shape as a handful of corporations are laying down the infrastructure necessary to position themselves as online global television-like services or "networks" into the future.

What is a major television network? At its core, it is a "platform" that has been created to enable video content to be pushed from a single point to a large audience. Blumenthal and Goodeneough (2006, 2) define it like this:

> In the United States, a broadcast network is a branded collection of 100 to 200 local television (or radio) stations that promote and exhibit the same program schedule all day and much of the night. This system permits a television network to build national audiences for programs and performers. The primary revenue stream for these programs is the sale of audience access in the form of commercial time.

Brown (1977, 300) adds that TV networks are

> chains of stations interconnected for the efficient distribution of programs and advertising from a central source. Because the economies of scale permit more ambitious and expensive production than individual stations could normally afford, and because they tend to be highly promotable, network programs usually draw greater audiences than local shows in any TV market.

The key to the commercial success of any free-to-air television network is the ability to cover all key city markets and deliver a national audience to advertising sponsors (Lieberman and Esgate 2002). However, the organisational mission may differ from purely commercial goals to political party propaganda and different business models exist and co-exist ranging from state-controlled networks subsidised by governments, public broadcasting services like PBS that rely on philanthropic donors to the commercial FTAs that dominate national markets and Murdoch's giant pay TV interests that operate in many markets.

The common elements appear to be:

▸ the ability to broadcast nationally to all major markets/cities;
▸ resources to commission or acquire content with audience appeal;

DOI: 10.1057/9781137326454

▸ a diverse slate of programming "pushed" from a central point;
▸ audiences in all markets view the same schedule of programming;
▸ a national audience with a broad demographic to attract sponsors;
▸ advertising sponsors prepared to pay for airtime to promote brands or alternatively other forms of sponsor (for example, government) prepared to pay for the cost of programming and/or the cost of running the network;
▸ economies of scale that facilitate both efficient program distribution and cost-efficient national advertising for sponsors;
▸ community reputation of high standing/value, that is, brand equity;
▸ marketing that effectively promotes the network and programs;
▸ capability to mount one-off high quality/content events.

We use the term global to mean a video service with actual or potentially broad transnational reach that provides a wide variety of content. Our focus is on transnational on-demand online television-like services either via web browsers or set-top boxes (for example, Apple TV, Google TV and Roku) or via apps or web browsers on tablet computers, games consoles, smart phones, computers or Internet-enabled Smart TVs. Chapters 4 and 5 discuss the leading "post-Hollywood" distribution "majors" that have emerged as contenders seeking to establish themselves online as potential screen networks:

▸ Google/YouTube and its ecosystem are the potential front-runners, and for that reason the next chapter is dedicated to its strategy;
▸ Apple's ecosystem, comprising iTunes, iMac, MacBook, iPad, iPod, iPhone, Apple TV, iCloud and possibly the rumoured iTV;
▸ Amazon's eco-system, comprising Amazon Studios, CreateSpace, Amazon Instant Video, LoveFilm, Amazon Cloud, Kindle Fire, Withoutabox and IMDb;
▸ and Yahoo!, Facebook, Netflix and Hulu (the only Hollywood-owned company among the third wave leaders).

It is obvious that, by virtue of their multi-national and aspirationally global reach, these players do not meet key criteria for a TV network. They may not meet others. We comment on this in the next chapters. What they may be doing, however, is remaking the criteria for future TV networking.

Why, though, only these players? One could also argue that the BBC, through BBC Worldwide and BBC iPlayer, also provides a global

DOI: 10.1057/9781137326454

television service within these terms. It does to some extent, except that users with UK IP addresses have free access to a deeper library via iPlayer than those in other countries, and the latter also have to pay a subscription fee. The BBC's Project Barcelona aims to digitise substantial BBC back catalogue and make it available as a streaming service.

The sheer size and scale of the newly merged Youku and Tudou in China perforce places them within the borders of potentially globally influential players. However, theirs is an exclusively national focus and thus we have treated them, in Chapter 2, as the single major force in rest-of-the-world developments.

A case could also be argued that News Corporation already provides global-reach TV services (including online catch-up television) via Fox in the US, Star in Asia, Sky in Europe and Foxtel in the South Pacific. However, News Corporation's global reach is based on iterating a proven but traditional pay-TV formula within bounded jurisdictions.

Other networks like ESPN (a Disney-owned company), CNN (Time-Warner owned), HBO GO and Deutsche Welle offer niche services to Internet users around the world, rather than a wide and varied slate of general programming to match a traditional television network. Other online distribution services with global reach that could also evolve and become part of the club are rooted in Hollywood: Crackle (Sony), UltraViolet (DECE's cloud based virtual video service) and Disney's rival digital locker KeyChest.

DOI: 10.1057/9781137326454

4
The Players, Part One: YouTube/Google

Abstract: *Through their sheer size and global reach, YouTube and its owner Google have unquestionably emerged as the front-runner in online distribution and as a emerging TV-like network. This chapter provides an overview of the four main areas of professionally produced, or pro–am, content YouTube now operates in: YouTube's 100 channels original programming initiative, YouTube Live, YouTube Partners program and YouTube Movies. We conclude that the scope and scale of YouTube mean that its viewership is potentially global and reaches a broader demographic and cultural mix than any other major screen network does. Its comprehensive range of genres is underpinned by a capacity to commission original content and develop a diverse slate.*

Keywords: Google; YouTube; future of TV networks

Cunningham, Stuart and Silver, Jon. *Screen Distribution and the New King Kongs of the Online World*. Basingstoke: Palgrave Macmillan, 2013. DOI: 10.1057/9781137326454.

DOI: 10.1057/9781137326454

This chapter is devoted to an analysis of the powerhouse of online distribution – YouTube and its owner Google. Through its sheer size and global reach YouTube has in our view unquestionably emerged as the front-runner of online distribution as a global TV-like network. We continue this discussion in Chapter 5, where we profile Google's three main rivals for web supremacy – Amazon, Apple and Facebook, as well as three of the most important emerging players in the online distribution/Internet television space – Hulu, Netflix and Yahoo!

Google's stated mission is "to organise the world's information and make it universally accessible and useful" (2013). Chairman and CEO Eric Schmidt sees the company as providing platforms that enable content owners to find audiences (McDonald 2011). Google owns and operates three major video platforms, and its sites (driven by YouTube) are the largest video properties with a market share of 35% of all online video consumed in North America (comScore 2012). Google TV seamlessly integrates Google's Chrome browser, YouTube and Google Play to enable users to locate video content on the web in the same way that Google's standard search engine retrieves information. It is available as either a software platform pre-installed in Smart TVs or as a set-top box connected to a TV. Google TV also integrates available online TV shows and movies from cable, satellite, network television, IPTV and Internet television, enabling users to find and watch on their television set any available content from those sources. GooglePlay, Google's response to iTunes, is an online digital store offering Hollywood movies for rental, along with music, games and apps.

YouTube

YouTube began life as a video sharing platform for user-generated content (UGC) and, despite heavy investment and the focus on developing professionally made content that will attract advertisers, the popular perception of YouTube as primarily a UGC site remains. Since 2009 however, YouTube has implemented a strategic plan to transform itself and reposition the site as a global TV platform. It redesigned the site into a personalised directory format in late 2011, and now enables users to choose channels of content they want to appear on their personalised home page.

In terms of professionally produced content, YouTube now operates in four main areas: YouTube's 100 channels original programming initiative,

YouTube Live, YouTube Partners program and YouTube Movies. In Chapter 6, we look qualitatively at the degree of experimentation and diversity seen in the original programming initiative.

YouTube's 100 channels original programming initiative was an investment of $100 million to commission about 25 hours per day of professionally produced, original programming to play exclusively on YouTube (Sweney 2011). It was provided to content creators as a loan covering start-up costs for the 100 new channels. YouTube invested another $200 million in order to market the new original content as an incentive to attract advertising. The original 100 channels included several Hispanic channels and covered 19 categories of content ranging from news and current affairs, to entertainment, sport, live variety shows and comedy. Studios behind the channels ranged from top-tier Hollywood talent to emerging producers from YouTube's Partners program. Investment levels varied with some top-tier channels attracting up to $5 million to cover their start up costs (Efrati and Schuker 2011; Hustvedt 2011a; Marshall 2011; Waugh 2011).

Under the investment arrangements, YouTube recoups start-up costs from revenues earned, thereafter splitting revenue 55:45% in favour of content creators (Marshall 2011). YouTube retains an 18-month exclusive window on content, after which time studios can shop the content to other distribution platforms which, after a three-year run, have the option to remove the content from YouTube if they wish (Efrati and Schuker 2011; Marshall 2011). After one year of operation, 25 of the original channels were averaging over 1 million views weekly, and the number of viewer subscriptions had doubled year-on-year (Kryncl 2012). In 2012 YouTube announced that it would fund 60 additional new channels – 15 from the United States, 18 from the United Kingdom (including 2 new original channels from the BBC), 11 from France and 9 from Germany (Gutelle 2012a).

The major TV networks' annual renewal/non-renewal rate of prime-time TV shows – where 65% of new shows "get axed" and only 35% are renewed for a second season (Roettgers 2012b), was mirrored by YouTube. It announced that it would reinvest only in 40% of the original 100 channels while allowing unfunded channels to continue broadcasting under their own steam. Jamie Byrne, YouTube's Director of Content Strategy, indicated that YouTube was "most concerned about engagement – primarily the total 'watch time' a channel has generated – and cost – how efficient programmers have been with their programming

DOI: 10.1057/9781137326454

budget". Byrne's indication that financial performance was not currently the primary focus has been seen as "a tacit acknowledgement that advertising for the channels remains a work-in-progress" (Kafka 2012a).

YouTube has invested heavily in developing its live broadcasting platform, *YouTube Live*. It has broadcast a growing number of high profile concerts and events including "Hope for Haiti", a globally broadcast charity concert attracting 600,000+ views (http://www.youtube.com/watch?v=P9AJunhGpcg); a U2 concert that attracted 10 million live streams (Parrack 2009b); the Alicia Keys benefit concert, "Keep a Child Alive", commemorating World AIDS Day; and a five-concert series from Madison Square Garden, which featured a live show by Arcade Fire, sponsored by American Express and streamed simultaneously on Vevo (Lawler 2012). YouTube Live has also broadcast large scale sporting events, such as the free streaming of Indian Premier League cricket (IPL) matches over 45 days to an audience of 50 million viewers – 40% of which were from outside India (Parrack 2010; Timmons 2010). Seven advertisers including Coca Cola and Hewlett Packard sponsored the IPL. Meanwhile, a deal with Japan's Major League Baseball (MLB) for live broadcasts of games to be streamed free, supported by ads "represents the largest partnership for premium sports content in YouTube history" (Marx and Gould 2010). In 2011, YouTube also broadcast live, all stages through to the cup final of the Copa America – the major continental FIFA soccer tournament for South America.

Other YouTube Live programming has included the variety show, *My Damn Channel LIVE*, which is broadcast live from its New York studio each day between 16:00 and 16:30 EDT (Cohen 2012a), as well as the occasional high profile political interview. President Obama's post-State of the Union interview and a conversation with US Speaker of the House John Boehner were streamed in 2011 (Timmons 2010). Recent live streams included the 2012 London Olympics and ParaOlympics, the Hajj and Ramadan prayers, and US election events such as the 2012 Democratic and GOP conventions and US Presidential debates.

As the following snapshot of YouTube Live taken on 9 May 2012 at midday (Australian Eastern Standard Time) reveals, YouTube remains a relatively open platform. It is comprised of a mix of professional, pro–am and amateur content from around the world, that was broken down into the categories of "Live Now", "Upcoming – next 24 hours", "Next 7 Days", "Recently Broadcasted" and "Featured Live Events". Most

DOI: 10.1057/9781137326454

of the 71 programs that were listed as "Live Now" were live, but some had finished their stream. There was representation from Japan, Korea, India, Spain, the US, Russia and Eastern Europe, as well as 24 programs from the Middle East. Forty live programs were listed as "Upcoming in the next 24 hours" and 33 were listed as coming in the "Next 7 days". Additionally, 27 programs of varying genres and quality were listed as "Recently Broadcasted" and three events were "Featured Live". Table 4.1 shows a small selection from that snapshot illustrating the variety of content, scope and scale of productions and audience reach in video views.

YouTube Partners program is a grow-your-own nursery for budding producers and an incubator for next-generation content creators. Google acquired Next New Networks (NNN), a pace-setting online TV network that "has come as close as anyone to cracking the code on how to create winning web programs and generate huge audiences" (Richmond 2011). NNN now operates the *YouTube Next* program and is responsible

TABLE 4.1   *Selected examples of YouTube Live at 1200 Australian Eastern Standard Time, 9 May 2012*

Channel	Event	Subscribers	Video views
Play On Network	2012 FHSAA 5A Softball Championship Final	1,605	1,299, 633
Melody Aflam	Classic and modern Arabic movies	18,542	2,249,040
Alnas TV	Arabic current affairs program with live audience phone-ins	23,172	5,065,163
Sports Gaming Universe	SGU Live Stream	13,951	3,348,316
TBS Newsi	Tokyo Broadcasting System News Portal	25,520	65,785,409
Al Jazeera	Al Jazeera English Live	252,370	367,313,213
GazGolder Official (Russian)	VideoGaz (live music)	95,686	83,480,138
Dan McDermott	News & Tech Tuesday	143	11,734
Fashion TV Direct	Fashion TV	15,156	5,978,109
Makkah Live	Makkah Live – The Haj	27,641	139,492
Final Fantasy IX Channel	Live – Vana'diel	5,014	1,435,312
LBC	Basketball	4,903	9,640,015
ONtv	ONtv livestreaming Arabic talk show	82,855	34,728,219

DOI: 10.1057/9781137326454

for mentoring partners' development through educational programs to professionalise their production skills and teach them strategies to find audiences and monetise their content. The Sophomore Initiative *Next Up* brought together selected producers of cooking and training programs in four-day, virtual boot camps called *Next Chef* and *Next Trainer*, where they received $5,000 worth of equipment, access to mentoring, filming and editing lessons and $10,000 promotion on YouTube (Cohen 2011; Cohen 2012b). *Next Cause* targeted not-for-profit organisations by training them to make better use of online video (Baldwin 2012a). *Next Vlogger* selected 16 participants for a three-month program of "intimate educational workshops" and provided them with $5,000 worth of video equipment and $10,000 worth of promotion on YouTube. They were also given access to mentoring by iJustine, one of YouTube's most successful Vloggers with nearly 250 million views worldwide (Baldwin 2012b). Another talent search *Next EDU Gurus* identified ten innovative educators from the US, Canada and the UK who YouTube would fund to develop new science, history and foreign language channels (Gutelle 2012b).

In 2011, YouTube had 15,000 partners earning revenues from the display ads being placed next to or within their videos and by making their videos available for rental. Hundreds of those partners earned more than $1,000 per month from the program. The rate of uptake and returns for partners has been growing rapidly (Morrison 2011). By October 2012, over 1 million channels were part of Partners program. In total, they had over 500 million subscribers and 251 billion video views. YouTube Partners were reaching the 100,000 subscribers milestone at five times the rate they were achieving two years earlier (Kryncl 2012), and 78 channels had in excess of 1 million subscribers (Shey 2012).

YouTube Movies is a digital store for renting premium Hollywood content. Google invested $100–200 million to supply movies to both YouTube Movies and Google Play (Google's response to the Apple iTunes store). While growing rapidly, the entire library is not globally available. In Australia, for example, a 9 May 2012 catalogue count of YouTube Movies revealed that only 174 movies were visible for rental on the site; on offer were a mix of titles from recent blockbusters to B-grade back catalogue films. However, six months later, by 29 November 2012, the available library had grown to include thousands of on-demand movies covering 19 genres ranging from Hollywood blockbusters to documentaries and short films, including over 1,000 world cinema and Bollywood films, and over 1,000 free movie titles.

DOI: 10.1057/9781137326454

Google's strategy

Horan and Rayport (2011) argue that Google is locked in an overall struggle for Web dominance with Amazon, Apple and Facebook. It has both the infrastructure and resources to become a major player in Internet television and to seriously challenge the industry dominance of the major TV networks and Hollywood. Google has size, scope and scale: during 2011, its assets included $39 billion in cash, coupled with an annual free cash flow of $9.4 billion (by comparison, the entire annual box office at North American movie theatres was $10.2 billion in 2011). Google is also the largest advertising platform in the world, with an ecosystem that includes Google TV, YouTube, Chrome (the most widely used web browser worldwide), Gmail (the most widely used web-based email provider worldwide), Android phone operating systems, the telecommunications equipment corporation Motorola Mobility (Zibreg 2011) and in 2011, Google Chrome became the OS for Chromebook laptops and touch screen devices from Samsung and Acer.

Taking Google's acquisitions and innovations since 2006 in conjunction with YouTube's ambitions and strategies, it is arguable that Google/YouTube aspires to dominate Internet television and seriously challenge North American network television for viewership and advertising revenues. Google's first foray into online video with Google Video was quickly eclipsed by the phenomenal rise of YouTube. As video began to proliferate across the web, YouTube was seen as a good strategic fit with Google's stated mission "to organise the world's information and make it accessible" and, unable to compete, Google acquired YouTube.

Its second venture into online video came with the launch that same year of an online video store offering movie downloads and rentals. Launched in 2006, the venture lasted little more than 12 months (Tyler 2006, Screen Digest 2007). Larry Page, Google's co-founder said: "For video producers and anyone with a video camera, Google Video will give you a platform to publish to the entire Google audience in a fast, free and seamless way" (Tyler 2006). But Google Video quickly failed, primarily because the major studios in Hollywood refused to supply premium content to the platform. It was dead by late 2007.

The third video platform Google launched was Google TV in 2010. It was software that could either be embedded within certain next generation TVs from partnering brands, or could alternatively be purchased as an

DOI: 10.1057/9781137326454

add-on set top box connected to a TV with HDMI inputs. The key advantages of Google TV are that it not only transforms a "dumb" into a smart TV by adding Internet functionality through Google Chrome, but it also provides a powerful video search engine capable of finding and bringing content from any source on the Web (cable, satellite, Network TV, Netflix, Hulu, Amazon, YouTube etc) – ranging from high quality commercial programming to user-generated content, directly into the user's living room or onto their Android device. At its launch, Google TV's product manager, Rishi Chandra, remarked on the annual $70 billion spend on television advertising within the US, and to 4 billion TV viewers worldwide (Chandra 2010). Considering Google's core business revenues are based on advertising, Chandra's message was clear: the company intended to try to win over some of TV's advertising dollars, backed by its belief that the future of the television market was online and global.

Two key concerns about Google TV have been raised by Hollywood and the TV network industry executives. Firstly, the platform has the potential to fuel increased online video piracy as "Google TV will not [...] filter out sites that offer pirated video streams" (Chmielewski and Guynn 2010). And secondly, by bringing the Web directly to the living room TV, "Google TV would encourage consumers to ditch their $70 monthly cable and satellite subscriptions in favor of watching video free via the Internet" (Chmielewski and Guynn 2010). Indeed, Google TV was seen as such a threat that incumbents NBC, ABC and Viacom (CBS) blocked content.

Attempting to allay such fears, Google Chairman Eric Schmidt stated that Google TV's intent was to "support the content industry by providing an open platform for the next generation of TVs to evolve" (McDonald 2011). Schmidt added that the company had "neither the ambition nor the know-how to actually produce content on a large scale, the firm's focus is on providing platforms for people to engage with content" (McDonald 2011). Nevertheless, the *Wall Street Journal* reported that "some TV and cable executives have said privately they viewed Google's moves as a threat to their business. TV networks have blocked the programming that they offer online, from Google TV" (Efrati and Schuker 2011). And in the months prior to Google's announcement to invest $100 million in YouTube's Original Channels Initiative, the *Wall Street Journal* reported that:

> Google was spending a hundred million dollars to commission premium YouTube content from the likes of Creative Artists Agency, William Morris Endeavour and International Creative Management, to name a few. But the

search monster's agenda is likely much, much bigger, according to a research note issued to clients by William Blair & Company. The firm believes that Google is silently buying/licensing hundreds of millions of dollars of professional Hollywood content [...] Google has made several key Hollywood hires over the past year to understand content rights. (Zibreg 2011)

Google's strategy can also be seen in its negotiations for the acquisition of Hulu (Guynn and Chmielewski 2011). Google was one of the final bidders – along with Amazon, Yahoo and Dish Network – for Hulu, and is reported to have made the highest bid of $4 billion, albeit under terms that Hulu owners Comcast–NBC–Universal, Fox and Disney were not prepared to accept (Carlson 2011; Davis 2011; Greenberg 2011; Guynn and Chmielewski 2011). Consequently, "News Corp, NBC-Universal and Disney decided to take the joint venture off the auction block and run it for the foreseeable future" (Wallenstein 2011a).

Ultimately, the outcome of these various negotiations have resulted in premium Hollywood content being made available to rent on GooglePlay and through YouTube Movies, while Google TV offers a search engine that can not only find any online movie or TV content from legal sources, but has the capability to locate that content on torrent sites and YouTube. Google seeks to have all bases covered in the online video space. But what about YouTube?

Unlike Google's denials of being a threat to television incumbents, YouTube's senior executive team have not been reticent to hide their ambitions and goals, as evidenced by YouTube CEO Salar Kamangar's statement:

> I think the next set of media companies are going to be created on the web and that YouTube is going to be a big part of that. CNN was mocked at the start (Ted Turner's folly!), as was ESPN... We're helping define a new way for content creators to reach an audiences [...] We don't want to replicate what's out there, we want to bring to you the kind of content that you can't get on TV. (Vascellaro et al. 2011)

Learmonth (2011) argues that YouTube is creating the next generation of cable TV, built and scaled for the web: "Instead of 500-odd channels on TV, YouTube is making a play for the 'next 10,000', appealing to all sorts of niches and interest groups". Hunter Walk, YouTube's head of product, believes that YouTube is emerging as the first global TV station:

> Not only has YouTube created the largest online video community in the world, it's shaping the way video is produced, distributed and monetised

DOI: 10.1057/9781137326454

[…] We've built the technology platform, aggregated the audience, and now have the monetisation tools that allow anyone who wants to create and distribute content to do it successfully through a single point at a global scale. (in Sacks 2011)

Taken together, such statements – along with the various funding and content initiatives discussed in more detail in Chapter 6 – provide mounting evidence that YouTube is laying the foundations to provide a full Internet television-like package accessible to a potentially global audience. And whilst YouTube's core business is focused on the commercial TV model of advertising supported free content, other business models are being introduced, including streaming rentals through YouTube Movies and Subscription Video on Demand – SVOD (Szalai 2012a). Robert Kyncl, Global Head of Content said YouTube will "offer an option to all the channels that are our partners to start charging subscriptions for their content" (Vivarelli 2012).

YouTube has been transformed from a loss-making UGC-only video platform (when Google acquired it in 2006) to generating an estimated $3.6 billion annually in gross revenues in 2012, and Citigroup analyst Mark Mahany estimated that YouTube would earn net revenues of $2.4 billion after splitting the gross revenues with its partners (Kafka 2012b).

David Cohen, an executive vice president at advertising agency Universal McCann described the 100 Channel Initiative in the *Wall Street Journal* as "the most audacious original programming initiative for the Internet" (in Efrati and Schuker 2011). And, with funding models in place, programming on original channels such as WIGS and Machinima is edging towards major network status in terms of quality. WIGS, for example, has an online programming niche offering high-gloss drama for women and about women, attracting A-list talent such as Julia Styles, America Ferrera, Jennifer Beals and Maura Tierney who work at union-scale in short series – 3–15 episodes, averaging 8 to 9 minutes each (Hale 2012). *Battlestar Galactica: Blood and Chrome* and *Halo 4: Forward Unto Dawn* were big budget sci-fi series that premiered on the Machinma channel in 2012, the latter funded by Microsoft to the tune of $10 million as part of the marketing for the latest game in the Halo series (Edwards 2012).

YouTube (and Yahoo and Hulu) has even begun to mimic the behaviour of traditional TV and cable networks by holding their own advertising "Upfronts" for the coming "season" in which they presented their forthcoming slate of Web Original series to Madison Avenue advertising executives to garner their share of the annual advertising spend in TV media. An executive close to the deal said these series are distinct from the "channel" strategy usually pursued. Rather, they are pitched as branded entertainment that wouldn't get the go-ahead without a big-ticket advertiser attached (Learmonth 2011). Google also has a point of difference that provides competitive advantage to the traditional networks because its "pedigree in capturing and analysing user's likes and dislikes was something big broadcasters and cable channels such as HBO or Showtime cannot do" (Shiels 2011).

YouTube's current face both exemplifies and transforms what the term TV network means, as we canvassed it in the previous chapter. YouTube remains (thankfully) a platform for a gigantic grab-bag of content of enormous variety, and so "fails" the traditional TV network threshold tests for stabilised, filtered content. But its viewership is *potentially* global and reaches a broader demographic and cultural mix than any other major network does. Its 100-channels of professionally produced programming includes a comprehensive range of genres and is underpinned by a capacity to commission original content and a diverse slate. Both these elements may be attractive to advertisers because they have options to mount global campaigns, target specific markets (city, countries) or target specific users based on their past online behaviours.

Table 4.2 highlights the key milestones in the Google/YouTube story.

TABLE 4.2   *Google and YouTube key milestones*

Year		Milestone
2005	Jan	Google Video hosting site and video search engine launched
	Feb	YouTube video hosting/sharing platform launched
2006	July	Rapid growth – YouTube announced 65,000 videos uploaded daily &100 million views streamed daily
	Nov	Google acquires YouTube
2007	June	YouTube made available on Apple mobile devices
2008	Nov	YouTube launches Shows as competition for Hulu offering free MGM, LionsGate and CBS TV shows and movies supported by advertising
	Nov	YouTube adds 750p HD quality support & widescreen
2009	Jan	YouTube streaming video becomes available on leading set-top boxes, media players, browsers and games consoles
	Jan	Google Video Store launched
	Oct	Live U2 concert broadcast on YouTube gets 10 million views

Continued

DOI: 10.1057/9781137326454

TABLE 4.2   *Continued*

Year		Milestone
	Nov	YouTube launches Shows in UK with 4,000 titles and 60 partners. YouTube adds 1080p HD support
	Dec	YouTube streams live Alicia Keys "Keep a Child Alive" concert for World AIDS Day
2010	Jan	YouTube launches film rental service – 6,000 movies
	Jan	Live concert "Hope for Haiti" broadcast on YouTube
	Mar	YouTube streams Indian Premier League Cricket – the first worldwide free online broadcast of a major sporting event. YouTube achieves 50 million viewers over 45 days with 40% streaming from outside India
	May	YouTube delivers 14 billion videos in May = 43% market share of all online video streamed in the US
	Aug	YouTube broadcasts first-of-five live American Express-sponsored concert series from New York giving viewers interactive control over preferred camera angles
	Oct	Google TV launched as a smart TV platform integrating Android & Chrome browser for video search, with the tagline "TV meets the Web, the Web meets TV"
2011	Mar	YouTube acquires web TV company Next New Networks for $49.4 million (Morrison 2011)
	Apr	30% of YouTube videos account for 99% of all views
	Apr	Google announces its free video hosting service will cease and hosted videos will be migrated to YouTube
	Apr	Google secretly licensing $100–200 million of premium movie & TV content via top Hollywood talent agencies
	May	YouTube served 2 billion videos per day with 3 billion views per day
	May	Google, Dish, Amazon and Yahoo! bid to buy Hulu, with Google's $4 billion the highest bid
	May	Disney–YouTube co-production investment $15 million of original content for Disney.com YouTube channel
	June	Google Chrome becomes the OS for Samsung Chromebook laptops
	Oct	YouTube announces $100 million of professionally produced original content covering 19 genres across 100 new channels
2012	Jan	YouTube has 800 million unique viewers per month
	Mar	GooglePlay launched to provide direct competition to Apple's iTunes and Amazon using Google's Android operating system
	Mar	GooglePlay merges its Android market (apps) with Google Video, and Google Music into one online store featuring movies, books, music and apps, offering Premium Hollywood via VOD

Continued

DOI: 10.1057/9781137326454

TABLE 4.2   *Continued*

Year		Milestone
	Mar	YouTube streams first live daily variety show My Damn Channel Live! every Wednesday in regular 4pm–4:30pm EST timeslot
	May	YouTube announces $200 million investment to market Original channels at the first ever Digital Content NewFront
	July	A studio (YouTube Creator Space) opens in London
	July	4 million creative content-licensed videos now on YouTube
	July	Official IOC YouTube channel streams Olympics live
	Oct	YouTube announces funding for 60 new Original channels and 53 are international from UK, France and Germany
	Oct	YouTube's Global Head of Content indicates Partners will be offered the option of charging subscriptions for some content
	Nov	YouTube decides to continue funding only 40% of its programming deals with the first 100 Original channels
	Nov	1 million YouTube Partners come from 27 countries
	Nov	70% of YouTube traffic is from outside the US
	Nov	A second studio (YouTube Creator Space) opens in L.A.
2013	Feb	Third YouTube Creator Space studio for Partners opens in Tokyo
	Feb	YouTube announces plan for 2013 opening of fourth studio in New York
	Feb	Google to challenge Microsoft, with Chrome touchscreen laptops
	May	30 premium YouTube channels convert to monthly paid subscription model.

DOI: 10.1057/9781137326454

5

The Players, Part Two: Rivals in Online Distribution

Abstract: *Six companies are profiled: Amazon, one of the largest Internet companies with a production and distribution ecosystem of great scale and potential; Apple, whose customer-centric, marketing-oriented approach has provided it with the scale and resources to engage its massive user base should it so choose; and Facebook, which, as it encounters increasing competition in the social network space may need to differentiate itself from rivals in order to retain its stickiness as a destination for existing users and to continue to attract new users. In addition, Yahoo! adheres to a typical Hollywood strategy of signing big name talent and developing programming built around that talent; Netflix is the recognised market leader in streaming movie and TV rentals and has recently committed to commissioning content; and Hulu is the incumbent TV networks' major play in the online video space.*

Keywords: future of TV networks; online screen distribution; Apple; Amazon; Netflix; Yahoo!; Facebook; Hulu

Cunningham, Stuart and Silver, Jon. *Screen Distribution and the New King Kongs of the Online World*. Basingstoke: Palgrave Macmillan, 2013. DOI: 10.1057/9781137326454.

While Google's YouTube platform clearly dominates the online video market in terms of share of viewers and video streams, there are several other key players whose strategy, resources and capabilities could also see them emerge as global TV-like networks. The first three cases discussed in this chapter focus on Google's main rivals for web supremacy – Amazon, Apple and Facebook. The final three cases focus on three of the most important emerging players in the online distribution/Internet television space – Hulu, Netflix and Yahoo!

Amazon

Amazon is one of the largest and most dominant Internet companies with sufficient financial depth, scope and scale (massive global customer base) and technology (Kindle devices, Cloud services) to emerge as a global player in Internet television. It has been quietly constructing a vertically integrated production–distribution–exhibition platform for online distribution that could be leveraged to provide a global Internet television service. The core components are:

▸ Production – Amazon Studios consists of script development and production, including a first look deal with Warner Brothers and a co-production agreement should Warner decide to proceed with any acquisitions;
▸ Distribution – Amazon.com sells film and television DVDs and BluRays; Amazon Cloud is one of the largest Cloud service provider operations on the Internet, providing 20% of the Web's cloud services (Levy 2011); Withoutabox represents the Internet's largest global matchmaking service for filmmakers and film festivals; IMDb.com is an online film & TV industry directory that also provides online film marketing/publicity on a fee-for-service basis;
▸ Distribution/Exhibition – Amazon Instant Video digital store offers streaming movies & TV on demand in the US while Amazon's European subsidiary LoveFilm streams movies and TV programs on that continent; another subsidiary CreateSpace is a self-publishing platform for aspiring filmmakers, musicians and authors; Amazon's app store for Android features apps providing film, TV and other video content; Kindle Fire is a video tablet

DOI: 10.1057/9781137326454

computer enabling customers to stream movies and TV; Instantly Watch is an embedded app on a range of HDTVs and BluRay players (LG, Panasonic, Sony and Vizio), set top boxes (Roku, Logitech and Sony media players) and Sony PS3 game console. Amazon's Instant Video streaming library is available free to Amazon customers who pay for $79 per year for the Amazon Prime delivery service in the US.

Although the bulk of Amazon's activities in this arena are focused on the sale and rental of high-end Hollywood film and TV programs, Amazon. com, CreateSpace, Withoutabox and LoveFilm all offer open access pathways for aspiring and independent filmmakers. But this relatively passive provision of platforms has turned into active sourcing with three interesting developments in script development and streaming video. The first was the launch of Amazon Studios – an open platform user-generated online development and production studio that crowdsources the development process of scripts until they are production-ready (Groves 2010). Under the leadership of Hollywood insider Roy Price (son of Frank Price, a former President of Universal), Amazon Studios aims to "discover great talent and produce programming that audiences will love" (Amazon Studios 2012). Amazon Studios aims to discover and foster talent from around the world (Amazon Studios 2012).

Amazon Studios' plan to produce episodic TV resulted in 809 projects uploaded and under review by December 2012, with 13 series selected for development and 34 "notable projects" still under consideration. The studio also formed the People's Production Company (PPC) and solicited scripts for original web TV series, paying $10,000 to option projects and $55,000 if the show is made, plus royalties. PPC will produce these programs and they will be distributed on the Amazon Instant Video platform. The aim, according to Price, is to develop shows with the look and feel of real TV shows, and with commensurate production budgets (Kafka 2012c). As the original focus for Amazon Studios was on feature length content, developments here have advanced even further. As of December 2012, 23 projects are in-development, and 26 more are under consideration. In addition, a total of 836 scripts have been submitted, 576 trailers have been through audience testing, and 579 films have actually been market-tested.

A further development worth consideration was Amazon's decision to bid for Hulu. Amazon expressed interest in Hulu for two reasons: firstly,

DOI: 10.1057/9781137326454

to provide guaranteed Hollywood content for Amazon Prime's instant video streaming service; and secondly, to provide content for its Kindle Fire video tablet. The acquisition of Hulu would have strengthened Amazon's competitive position against both Apple TV but more importantly, against the iPad.

Finally, an important development for Amazon in terms of online television can be seen in the increasing focus on securing film and TV content exclusively for Amazon Instant Video and its European subsidiary LoveFilm. A deal with Warner Brothers in the UK to exclusively stream WB Movies on LoveFilm effectively created a second Pay TV window (following the first Pay TV run on BSkyB). Warner is also launching an exclusive movie channel of older films on the LoveFilm platform (Dawtrey 2011).

While the pieces of Amazon's long-term strategy for online television have yet to form a clear picture, it is evident that Amazon is emerging as a web content powerhouse. While almost half its revenues come from sales of media like books, music, TV shows and movies, Jeff Bezos (Chairman and CEO) claims Amazon studios to be a totally new way of making movies and TV shows, and that with Kindle Fire, Amazon has developed "a fully integrated media service" that leverages on Amazon's own cloud service operation (Levy 2011). The sheer scope and scale of its ecosystem and its film and television-related businesses signals that Amazon has infrastructure falling into place to emerge as a major media company with the ability to offer a global Internet television-like service as an alternative to traditional television.

Apple

Historically Apple's core business was focused on the development of user-friendly computers. Steve Jobs' return to Apple in 1996 helped redefine Apple, transforming it from a post-Jobs product-driven company with weak distribution and ineffective marketing into a customer-centric, marketing-oriented manufacturer of portable media players and mobile computers. At the heart of this strategy is the Apple iTunes store, a hub for video, music, e-books, apps and other audio-visual content for consumers to screen on iMac, iPod, iPad, iPhone and Apple TV. Apple's sophisticated marketing expertise and innovative devices enabled it to achieve market-leader status in the smart phone and tablet markets.

DOI: 10.1057/9781137326454

Central to Apple's success was the implementation of the iTunes micropayment system coupled with a platform that engages a huge user base. With iTunes strategically underpinning the success of that whole eco-system, the acquisition of desirable content is key to satisfying owners of those devices, and to selling more devices. iTunes is not an open-access platform like YouTube. Independent creators of film and television – with occasional exceptions – need to find content aggregators that have strategic relationships to supply Apple in order to appear on iTunes. And the focus for content acquisition is Hollywood. At a 2010 product launch Steve Jobs stated that "what have we learned from our users [...] is, the number 1, 2 and 3 thing they want is Hollywood movies and TV shows whenever they want them – it's that simple. They want Hollywood movies and TV shows, they don't want amateur hour".

While Apple has yet to show interest in commissioning original content in its own right, indicators of possible longer-term ambitions in the online distribution space may lie in three developments: Firstly, CBS CEO Lester Moonves confirmed that he had been approached by Steve Jobs about an SVOD service: "he met with Jobs, the late Apple CEO, and heard a pitch for what was billed as a subscription content service, but ultimately he said he wasn't interested in providing CBS shows or films to the venture" (Belloni 2012). Secondly, the UK's *Daily Telegraph* and others reported that Apple was rumoured to be considering bidding for the English Premier League TV rights which if true, would likely indicate Apple was planning an online subscription streaming service (Richmond 2012; Sale 2012). Thirdly, around the same time Apple was also rumoured to be interested in bidding for Hulu (Fixmer and Satariano 2011; Sherr 2011; White 2011). While Apple did not enter a formal bid it signals – if true that it was considering the acquisition – a determination to secure premium TV content.

Steve Jobs' public statement on Apple's commitment to Hollywood content and his desire to add a subscription service indicate that Apple was not trying to compete with Hollywood's major content creators. Apple's strategy to-date is based on distribution and retailing via the integration of its iTunes-driven ecosystem with its popular mobile devices that together reach a huge online audience. Consumers can stream content either by renting or buying directly from iTunes or via apps on their iPads or iPhones or Apple TV for services such as Netflix, Hulu Plus, Amazon Instant Video in the US or LoveFilm, BBC iPlayer and Sky TV Now in the UK.

DOI: 10.1057/9781137326454

A cautionary lesson for Apple is that despite providing quality online distribution streaming solutions, device-led solutions like TiVo, Google TV and XBox have yet to massively impact the online TV market. iPad and iPhone are currently market leaders but as competition intensifies differentiation will likely become key to maintaining leadership. To do this, Apple has to stay ahead of the pack with high quality product innovation and maintain leadership through service differentiation. Faced with intensifying competition for the online video audience plus the ever-rising acquisition costs for Hollywood content, Apple might consider commissioning unique original programming as YouTube, Netflix and Hulu have already done to complement the introduction of any Apple TV subscription service. It certainly has the size, scale, resources and infrastructure already in place to engage its massive user base to become a serious longer-term alternative to traditional television should it so choose. It should not be forgotten that when Steve Jobs acquired Pixar in 1986 it was the graphics group of the computer division of LucasFilm. Jobs then branded it Pixar and bankrolled John Lassetter, transforming it into a major studio that made a series of blockbuster hits like *Toy Story*, before on-selling it to Disney. As part of that deal, Jobs sat on the Disney board and following his death, his widow remains Disney's largest individual shareholder. Thus creating premium content and understanding Hollywood is not totally unfamiliar territory for Apple.

Facebook

The world's most popular social network has over 1 billion users worldwide. While Facebook hosts user-videos and serves as a portal to other video content embedded on the site by third parties, like Google and YouTube it draws its major revenues from advertising. So why would Facebook be considered to be a potential candidate to emerge as a major online television network?

We argue that as Facebook encounters increasing competition in the social network space, in order to retain its stickiness as a destination for existing users and to continue to attract new users, it will need to clearly differentiate itself from rivals. Most video currently available on Facebook won't add sufficient value to Facebook's offering to provide an edge in the face of intensifying competition. During 2011–2012 the company leveraged its social interactivity and its micropayment system,

DOI: 10.1057/9781137326454

Facebook credits, to test the waters by offering movie, TV and original web series content to users.

A small number of films have been made available for streaming rental on Facebook, including *The Dark Knight* and *Abduction*, the latter being made available on the same day-and-date with the home video release (Szalai 2012b). In addition, Facebook has also seen a handful of limited theatrical movie releases launched simultaneously on the network including *Tomorrow, When the War Began* and *Marley* (a feature length documentary that had a limited theatrical release in the US and UK). It should be noted that Freestyle, the distributor of *Tomorrow, When the War Began*, also made the film available on iTunes, Vudu, Amazon and YouTube, partnering with video platform Milyoni for the Facebook release. If nothing else, Hollywood sees Facebook and its massive user base as a premium promotional channel. Thomas Gewecke, President of Warner Brothers Digital Distribution states that Facebook is "an increasingly influential destination for discovering and acquiring movie and television content" (Binazewski 2011).

Facebook has also experimented with original web series, with two exclusive – and consecutive – releases occurring in 2011. The first of these, *Aim High*, was a teen comedy from Warner Brothers Digital Distribution. *Aim High* was a cleverly constructed series leveraging Facebook's interactive potential to enable users to log into their personalised version of the series and to become part of the program as Facebook extracted relevant data from their personal profiles and embedded it into different points of the episode e.g. their name or image would appear in different scenes (Miller 2011). Whilst no narrative value is added to the series, the social bragging rights five seconds of fame might bring among friends watching on the social network remains significant. The second original series was an independently produced low-budget sci-fi series *Continuum* that utilised Facebook for a soft launch in order to stimulate awareness and interest and to try to build a fan base prior to its official premiere across multiple platforms in 2012. Within five days it had generated over 19,000 "likes" and had 5,400 "talking about this" on Facebook (Miller 2011).

In late 2011 Facebook launched FB TeeVee, announcing that it would comprise a combination of UGC and web original programming. It launched with 10 channels of original content and the target was for 75–100 channels by 2012. An inventory count eight months after the launch revealed FB TeeVee had 76 channels across 14 categories: Business & Finance (9 channels), Comedy (1), Education

(7), Entertainment (16), Fashion (3), Film & Animation (6), Food & Drinks (2), Health & Medicine (2), Music (12), News & Politics (3), People & Blogs (10), Science & Technology (2), Shopping (-) and Sports (3). The overwhelming impression of FB TeeVee is of low-grade UGC programming across the board.

While a lack of investment and focus has left minimal content resources for FB TeeVee, Facebook is still actively experimenting with ways to add value for users by combining movies and TV programs with its social networking infrastructure. Whilst Facebook has not yet commissioned any premium original content and lacks the sophisticated video platform capabilities that YouTube, Hulu, Netflix and others have, it certainly has the financial resources to develop competitive content if it so chooses. The most obvious entry point for Facebook is to continue to let others develop and test the market within its community using third party video platforms like Milyoni with its "Social Cinema" service (used for *Tomorrow, When the War Began*), its "Celebrity Cinema" service (used for *Marley*) and its "Social Live" streaming service for live concerts and sports. Should that new market yield results for Facebook, it could adopt Bebo.com's two-pronged strategy and negotiate program sponsorships to fund web originals, or alternatively act as a content aggregator and encourage content creators to employ branded entertainment and/or product placement strategies to pay for new original series. For content creators, the obvious benefit is the ability to build a community around a program through social networking strategies. With 1 billion users, a top ten place in video properties on the Web ranking, and around 50 million unique video viewers each month, the potential remains for good programming to quickly find a niche audience and realise opportunities for monetising content on Facebook. Whilst Facebook is not a first-mover in this space, contingent upon the success of YouTube and its key rivals, it is not hard to imagine a scenario where Facebook might become a later entrant.

Yahoo!

Pioneering portal Yahoo! has in recent years struggled, but despite its ongoing financial troubles and multiple changes of leadership (five CEOs in five years) it has diversified its business and has been a pace-setter in commissioning original programming for online audiences.

DOI: 10.1057/9781137326454

This strategy began during the six-year tenure of former CEO Terry Semel (ex-Chairman of Warner Brothers) and Lloyd Braun (former ABC Chairman) who failed to realise and deliver a vision they had announced of developing "smash-hit, medium defining programming" online (Elgin 2006). A second original programming strategy implemented in 2010 also failed despite hiring TV veterans to "produce TV-style content" (Ingram 2010). However, a third attempt has had some success. After establishing studio space in Manhattan in December 2012 and implementing its new Yahoo! Originals strategy, it climbed to the second spot on the US online video rankings when measured by unique viewers with a +20% rise in March on the previous month – 8 million extra viewers (Cohen 2012c).

Yahoo! adheres to a typical Hollywood talent-led strategy of signing big name talent (Tom Hanks, Ben Stiller, Bill Maher, Morgan Spurlock amongst others) and developing programming built around that talent. Yahoo! re-branded its online video portal YScreen!, offering multiple channels and a growing library of original web series across a range of genres. A catalouge-count on the YScreen! site on 18 May 2012 revealed a diverse slate of programming: Entertainment (4 Yahoo! originals and 30 other licensed shows); Comedy (7 Yahoo! original series); Lifestyle (16 Yahoo! originals + 11 other licensed shows); News (12 originals and 9 other shows); Sports (6 originals and 16 other licensed shows); Finance (4 originals and 9 other licensed shows).

Yahoo.com has long attracted high traffic volumes with 177 million unique monthly US visitors and in March 2012, it climbed to second position in the comScore Video Metrix chart for Top US online video content properties ranked by unique viewers (Cohen 2012c). And Yahoo!'s success with audiences is impressive, securing 21 out of the top 25 most-watched online series and drawing 61 million unique visitors who watch video on the site each month (Goldberg 2012). Yahoo! claims nearly all of the top 10 most-watched original series online, and the company finished first in 11 different content categories. Yahoo! outperformed brands in very competitive sectors, such as ESPN in sports and CNN in news (Wallenstein 2011b). Of the 47.3 million video streams Yahoo! generated in July 2011, Yahoo!'s original series alone garnered 27 million: significantly more than the 24.4 million video streams Hulu generated in its entirety for the same period (Wallenstein 2011b). Yahoo!'s hit web series of 2012 won best comedy and best actor in a comedy at the third annual Streamy Awards.

DOI: 10.1057/9781137326454

Yahoo! is capable of leveraging sophisticated data mining approaches to inform its program development choices. For example, heavy regular traffic on relationships-related content on the Yahoo! portal led to development of *Let's Talk About Love,* a new series featuring comedian Niecy Nash discussing "insights on all things romance". Access to such web analytics enables Yahoo! to refer viewers to thematically similar programming on the site, which is something that YouTube and Hulu cannot offer (Wallenstein 2011b).

Unlike other online video platforms where content is often branded entertainment and contingent upon sponsors paying production costs in-advance Yahoo!'s originals (like those of a TV network) have been firmly commissioned, signalling that Yahoo! is both committed and confident that its web originals will attract advertisers. And like YouTube and Hulu, Yahoo! also held digital upfronts in 2012 to present its forthcoming slate to Madison Avenue agency executives. It also announced it would market the slate with a launch event and promote the time that each of the new episodes actually premiere on YScreen as a means of boosting awareness of new shows (Wallenstein 2011b).

Clearly, Yahoo! is intent upon becoming and remaining a major player in Internet television. Consider its two previous failed attempts to establish its online TV platform in 2006 and 2010 taken in conjunction with its post-2011 strategy featuring a diverse range of programming and a level of commitment to produce web originals that have achieved success both with audiences and industry acclaim (many awards). Although Yahoo! was unsuccessful in its bid to buy Hulu, the decision to bid was a clear signal of its corporate intent in the online distribution space (Wallenstein 2011a).

Netflix

Netflix is the recognised market leader in streaming movie and TV rentals with its $7.99 all-you-can-watch monthly subscription service in North America. Its emergence from a financially troubled 2011 had been driven by an accelerated program of international expansion of the platform aiming to grow the subscriber base by pushing into Europe with launches in the UK and Ireland in January 2012 (TBI Vision 2012b), Sweden in October and Denmark, Norway and Finland by the end of 2012 (Gruenwedel 2012b). This followed earlier expansion into Canada

DOI: 10.1057/9781137326454

and 43 Latin American countries during 2010–2011. Further international expansion into Europe and Asia was likely based on an analysis of recruitment ads in which Netflix was "seeking linguists who can translate and customise marketing, user interface and content materials for the target market – Turkish, Dutch, Russian, French, Hindi, German, Italian, Danish, Korean, Finnish, Japanese and Spanish" (Roettgers 2011).

Netflix now has over 30 million subscribers worldwide streaming its VOD services: 25 million in North America and 5 million outside the US (Netflix.com 2012; Gruenwedel 2012c). Whilst it remains the streaming rental powerhouse in the US it faces intensifying competition from Hulu and Amazon Instant Video in the US market and very sophisticated competition for customers in Europe from Amazon's LoveFilm, in the UK from BSkyB (for premium movies) and terrestrial TV networks with high profile online presence (Roettgers 2011) and in Scandinavia from LoveFilm and Voddler.

Netflix recently concluded a deal whereby Oscar winning movie, *The Artist*, will make its pay TV debut "exclusively on Netflix rather than on traditional premium cable" (Szalai 2012c). This is a significant move because it signals that Netflix is willing to compete directly with cable TV for acquisition of premium content in order to differentiate its offerings in the market. In the DVD mail-order business, Netflix predominantly rented older catalogue titles and had limited access to new release movies because its release window followed the major video retailers, while premium TV programs went first to the major networks' own websites and to Hulu.

The $7.99 price-point for a monthly subscription is deemed critical for its future growth prospects but Netflix is faced with rising acquisition costs when renewing deals with the major studios in Hollywood. Its first real test came when Starz, a premium subscription channel and flagship service of Liberty Media, that had sub-licensed a VOD online streaming service comprising Hollywood studio movies and some original content to Netflix from 2008 to 2012, pressured Netflix to puts its titles in the premium tier of content and pass along those costs to subscribers. Netflix held firm and let the deal with Starz expire (Bricklin 2012).

Consequently, Netflix has committed to commissioning production of its own premium content to premiere in a first run in a Netflix-exclusive window before moving to VOD/home video release. Original content is seen as key to differentiating Netflix from the competition hence the need to grow its subscriber numbers quickly to balance rising acquisition

DOI: 10.1057/9781137326454

costs for content and to bankroll international expansion (Edwards and Yablon 2012). According to Chief Content Officer, Ted Sarandos, Netflix original programming will be of the highest quality and "indistinguishable from programs made for TV networks" (Owen 2012). This is borne out by the first five Netflix Originals announced so far: *House of Cards* starring Kevin Spacey and directed by David Fincher (Wallenstein 2011c; Wingfield and Schneider 2011); *Lillyhammer* (Kain 2012); a Netflix exclusive revival of the once popular Fox TV show *Arrested Development* (Flint 2011; Fritz 2012; Wallenstein 2011d; Wallenstein 2011e); *Hemlock Grove*, a ground-breaking gothic horror series starring Framke Janssen and a comedy entitled *Orange Is the New Black*.

What makes Netflix different from the incumbent TV networks is not only its increasingly global reach but its ability to leverage its customer analytics to inform its decision-making on customer offerings. Netflix debuted all eight episodes of *Lillyhammer* online while at the same time giving its customers the choice to watch the whole season in one session if they preferred, rather than being slaves to a weekly network TV schedule. Netflix used its intimate knowledge of "customers' ratings of past TV shows as a guide to steer them toward original programs like *Lilyhammer*" (Owen 2012). Terrestrial networks and cable TV don't have the depth of knowledge of their audiences' behaviours and preferences that offers competitive advantage to Internet companies like Netflix, Amazon, Hulu and Apple. Sarandos also indicated that Netflix enjoys another significant advantage over the incumbent networks in the form of much lower marketing costs because it will "use our traditional algorithms to bring attention to the show" (Wallenstein 2011c).

The success of Netflix has been perplexing for Hollywood because:

> Netflix is primarily in the business of aggregating content created by other companies and selling access to it as a subscription service to consumers. In a media culture committed to the proposition that "Content is King" the robust success of a mere re-distributor is something incomprehensible. (Knee 2011)

But it can be explained. The key to the company's rapid growth in the streaming market has been ubiquitous accessibility to the service via the Netflix app which is either embedded in or available for download to most smart TVs, games consoles, computers, tablets and other mobile and media streaming devices together with the fact that Netflix saw that the key to future subscriber growth was global and that to win the intensifying battle for the online audience it had to expand its platform internationally. It was the first-mover domestically and internationally in the now booming online distribution market. Netflix footprint already covers North, Central and South America, UK, Ireland and Scandinavia and it sent executives to visit Australia and Asia in 2012.

And with 30 million subscribers, "Netflix would have been the seventh most watched network inclusive of broadcast and cable networks ... it would also have been No 2 among cable networks" (Gruenwedel 2012d). Netflix is evolving into a global on-demand alternative-to-television service with the ability to reach consumers wanting streamed content on almost every screen that they want to watch it on.

Hulu

The meteoric rise of Hulu over a three-year period is well-documented but in real terms it ranked a distant second-placed market challenger behind Google/YouTube in the comScore Video Metrix rankings for March 2012 in the US market. However, as a joint venture between Comcast NBC–Universal, Fox and ABC–Disney it represents the incumbent TV networks major-play in the online video space. The owners had intended to sell Hulu at the end of the three-year joint venture agreement but took it off the auction block when they failed to get their asking price. Of the four bidders – Amazon, the Dish network, Google and Yahoo! – Dish tabled the highest acceptable offer at $1.9 billion but that was too low. Google offered $4 billion but wanted longer licenses. Hulu owners wouldn't agree to those terms (Rosoff and Carlson 2011; Greenberg 2011).

Three factors may have impacted the bids of the potential buyers and the decision not to sell. From the buyers' point-of-view, it was obvious that Hulu's owners preferred a subscription service like Hulu Plus. The relatively short duration of licensing agreements contained in the terms of the sale indicated that the TV networks would hike prices for licensing fees for content at the earliest opportunity. Higher acquisition costs for content were something Hulu was already facing under existing ownership. From the owners' point of view, whilst the failure to attract a buyer willing to acquire Hulu on their terms was disappointing, Google's bid, personally delivered by Larry Page, probably forced them to strategically re-think the wisdom of the sale:

here was a potential competitor with massive resources willing to pay $4 billion for a company in which they themselves could not really see the long-term value. What gives?

Add to that the fact that Hulu was for the first time bordering on the verge of profitability and Hulu Plus subscriptions were expected to account for more than half of Hulu's revenue in 2012. "There's no doubt that Hulu is becoming a more influential media business, with the company also revealing that its paid subscription base has reached 2 million and that 2012 revenue is on pace to far outstrip the $420 million grossed in 2011" (Frankel 2012). Hulu actually achieved 3 million Hulu Plus subscriptions and close to $700 million revenue in 2012 (Gutelle 2012c).

So what are Hulu's online ambitions? It expanded into Japan with a subscription-only service in 2011 (Hustvedt 2011b) and has publicly stated on its website that it plans to expand globally. It is transitioning from an ad-supported commercial television model for catch up TV and back catalogue programs, into a hybrid of free shows and paid subscriptions for more exclusive premium content through Hulu Plus. Hulu's mission is "to help people find the world's premium content when, where and how they want it". And faced with the prospect of rising content acquisition costs from its current owners and other TV major networks, Hulu decided to invest in commissioning its own premium content programming to differentiate it from other providers.

CEO Jason Kilar announced $500 million investment into original programming to be streamed exclusively on Hulu (Baldwin 2012c; Cohen 2012d). Like YouTube and Yahoo, Hulu employed traditional TV network strategy by holding its own digital television upfront with Madison Avenue advertising agencies to preview the 2012–2013 programming slate. At the upfront Hulu launched "a raft of new original series" (TBI Vision 2012a) and "like Netflix, Hulu is making a push into original series. It has also licensed 13 television shows that will appear exclusively online" (Chosick and Stelter 2012). Hulu had previously commissioned the 13-episode sitcom, *Battleground*, Morgan Spurlock's *A Day in the Life* that began life as a pilot on Fox, *Up to Speed* and it also acquired Shawn Doyle's *End Game*. Such activities represent "an indication of the role the new digital players like Hulu are beginning to have on funding original content" (Bulkley 2012; Landa 2012).

At a recent industry panel, Hulu's Senior Vice President of Content – Andy Forsell

DOI: 10.1057/9781137326454

let slip that Hulu is trying to make its original programming capable of winning major television awards. Whilst not a complete shocker, this tidbit is further indication that premium on-demand and over the Internet distribution-services-turned-studios are starting to see themselves as the new HBOs. (Landa 2012)

Whilst Hulu does not (yet) command an audience on the scale of YouTube, Facebook or Amazon, its expansion outside the US market into Japan signals that it believes that there is a global audience for its service. Its half-billion dollar investment in Hulu-commissioned original programming "capable of winning major TV awards" also signals corporate ambitions beyond its current status. This mimics the behaviour the pioneering cable TV networks but on a global scale. Hulu's focus remains solely on premium content; it is in no way a democratic platform like YouTube. Its future will be determined in 2013 following the departure of its founding CEO Jason Kilar. A contributing factor to Kilar's decision to move on from Hulu was that Hulu's three owners don't all share the same vision for the company. Will Hulu become a global TV-like network or will it transform into something more like the major networks' existing websites? Will its owners sell it or shut it down?

DOI: 10.1057/9781137326454

6
Does It Matter? The Content Question, and Conclusions

Abstract: *To what extent does having these new corporations increasingly control the flow of digital entertainment content change matters? The chapter documents and analyses the range of new content being commissioned for the new platforms. The book concludes by arguing that powerful players have entered the market, some of whom massively outrank in size and growth the companies which run film and television today. Like all large-scale corporations, they are likely to use market power to seek to limit competition and most will attempt to corral users inside walled gardens. But, through them, distribution of licit screen content has never before been so varied and accessible.*

Keywords: YouTube; Netflix; online distribution; screen distribution; film distribution; future of television; middle range theory

Cunningham, Stuart and Silver, Jon. *Screen Distribution and the New King Kongs of the Online World*. Basingstoke: Palgrave Macmillan, 2013. DOI: 10.1057/9781137326454.

DOI: 10.1057/9781137326454

How significant might all the change documented here be? From the point of view of media and communications studies, does it matter? Are we simply witnessing a possible changing of the guard of capitalist hegemons, with little change to the fundamental order of things? Or does the web and those born digital, "pure-play" enterprises which are coming to dominate its commercial dynamics, "change everything" (Gannes 2009)?

As we have suggested introducing this book, these, and many related, questions preoccupy scholarship and have attracted very substantial glass half-empty/half-full debates. The great theorist of the public sphere, Jürgen Habermas, seems unconvinced by claims to qualitative change for the better (2006). There is concern that researchers may be entirely "misunderstanding the Internet" (Curran et al, 2012), its potential and its implications. These significant authors in the discipline treat the impact of the Internet as a lower-order transformation that falls well short of the revolutionary political change wrought by the printing press.

We have adopted a middle range approach in this book, one that treats these questions as an invitation to empirical research, guided by a cultural politics that acknowledges that qualitative change, even progressive change, can occur out of the creative destruction driven by what Schumpeter (1934) called the capitalist "engine". Thomas Streeter, in his *The Net Effect: Romanticism, Capitalism, and the Internet* (2011) suggests that:

> If we want to understand the effect of that complex set of phenomena to which we attach the word Internet, we have to grasp it as a set of historical, contingent, and social processes, measured in significance by their productivity, by the ways in which they made a difference. (in Lee & Streeter 2012)

We can, in concluding the argument and summarising the evidence so far, ask a number of questions: what has been the rate of change in the screen distribution sector? What have new players brought to the sector? What new opportunities for content makers are there? A major focus of the chapter is to document the range of new content being commissioned by the increasingly TV network-like strategies of the major new platforms, and it to this that we turn first.

Content experimentation and diversity

In late 2012, we sampled a wide range of programming being commissioned as original content by the platforms discussed in Chapters 4 and 5 on the basis that this represents a central plank of the operation of a

DOI: 10.1057/9781137326454

TV network and is, without doubt, the most significant and very recent change in strategy of the new players. This amounted to 280 samples of television-like, studio quality production, comprising 168 YouTube programs/channels and 112 non-YouTube programs/channels. The YouTube videos are exclusively from its 100-channel major commissioning initiative. The rest are profiled on the basis of their offering innovation in genre, content and/or participants.

As a base level of fairly routine innovation, genre blending was common in the sample. We experience plenty of edutainment, infotainment and so on. Entertainment webcasts (music, film and gaming reviews, guides, and celebrity gossip) were the most prevalent, with 55 YouTube and 17 non-YouTube videos. This was followed by lifestyle shows, which included chat shows, how-to guides, beauty, food, shopping, women's interest and "Mom's TV". Lifestyle videos comprised 42 YouTube and 21 non-YouTube videos. Comedy (incorporating sit-com, stand-up, prank) provided 13 YouTube and 33 non-YouTube videos. Sports webcasts (25 YouTube and 11 non-YouTube), News and Current Affairs webcasts – including financial news – (6 YouTube and 16 non-YouTube) were also represented by a number of channels. Only YouTube had original Educational content, with 14 titles. Television-like drama series, small-scale webisodes through to full-scale programs like *House of Cards*, provided a total of 3 YouTube and 7 non-YouTube titles. There were also 7 non-YouTube documentary series.

The nomenclature for all this is different to mainstream TV. A "studio" (like Maker or Machinima) might have a number of networks (e.g., Maker Music, The Moms' View, Tutele). A YouTube "network" is a cluster of "channels" (e.g., Maker Music has 1516 Channels). A "channel" is a cluster of "videos" (e.g., The Polipop Channel – part of Maker Music – is a political chat channel with about 80 videos).

Also unlike broadcast television – with its time constrained 24-hour broadcast schedule – there is no simple format by which to measure the average length of an online TV webisode. Some streamed content from Netflix, Hulu and Yahoo! have consistent episodic run times (e.g., Netflix's *House of Cards* has 13x50 minute episodes). Some webisodes have fairly consistent run times, such as Felicia Day's *The Guild*, which has provided six seasons with episodes running anywhere between 4 and 10 minutes, averaging around 8 minutes. Other series have inconsistent run times: Jerry Seinfeld's *Comedians in Cars Getting Coffee* provided ten episodes running from 7 minutes to 17 minutes with an average of

11 minutes. Some comedic webisodes – such as *Annoying Orange* and *Bad Teeth* may be produced with mobile viewing in mind and run content that is consistently under 4 minutes.

YouTube

We concentrate on YouTube content and programming for the same reason that we have devoted a whole chapter to it previously – as the leading driver of substantive change. Par for the course, none of the examples we canvass now have been "locked up" as exclusive YouTube properties. All examples have been part of the YouTube Original Channel Initiative.

Outstanding examples of *popular entertainment experimentation* include *Halo 4: Forward Unto Dawn*, Machinima Prime studios, Maker studios and WIGS. *Halo 4: Forward Unto Dawn* is a stand-alone web series. It is a live-action sci-fi drama based on the successful Halo video game series that was funded through a $10 million investment from Microsoft (Edwards 2012) and is distributed by premium content channel Machinima Prime on YouTube. As of 28 November 2012, *Halo 4* had 10,021,489 video views. "We're either the best-funded web series of all time, a sort of mid-road healthy TV pilot, or a super-low-budget movie", said director Stewart Hendler (Edwards 2012). *Halo 4* is the first title in the franchise to be developed by 343 Industries, the Microsoft-owned studio that was tapped in 2007 to oversee the property after its creator, Bungie Studios, became independent and signed a ten-year publishing deal with Activision Blizzard. *Halo 4* won the 2013 Streamy Award for best drama series. The Streamy is the Emmy Award of the Web.

Machinima Prime is one of the early original channel initiatives, a channel/network that includes franchises *Battlestar Galactica: Blood and Chrome*, *Halo 4: Forward Unto Dawn*, *Daybreak* and *The Walking Dead: Torn Apart*. The Machinima Prime network also includes *Mortal Kombat: Legacy* – produced by Warner Brothers Digital Distribution. Machinima Prime is the 2nd ranked YouTube channel as of early 2013. Google has invested heavily in Machinima (Guglielmo 2012).

Maker studios is also an early original channels initiative, a channel/network with a progressive cachet. It produces several popular series and channels on YouTube including KassemG, Timothy DeLaGhetto, Peter Shukoff and Lloyd Ahlquist's *Epic Rap Battles of History*. It claims to have as many viewers as Nickelodeon (Miller 2011) at over 1 billion views per

DOI: 10.1057/9781137326454

month (Cohen 2012e; Manarino 2012) and 90 million subscribers (Graser 2012). Maker studies overtook the previously #1 ranked YouTube channel (Machinima) in October 2012 (Luo 2012). Put together, Maker studios combines 3,000+ channels, 120,000,000 subscribers, and 1,800,000,000 video views/month. It has partnered with Robert De Niro's Tribeca Enterprises, Kevin Smith (Silent Bob) and with Snoop Lion (Snoop Dogg). It received $36 million in investment funds from Time Warner in December 2012 (Gutelle 2012d).

There are some echoes of the wider and more political "maker movement", as charted by Chris Anderson (2012) in *Makers: The New Industrial Revolution,* in the claims made for Maker studios. COO Courtney Holt explained why the company was called Maker:

> It was all about the frustration. Traditional media you have this sort of pay-to-play, I own your assets, you're here as work for hire, and we tried to create something that's more of a mechanism to enable creators all over the world to "make things" as opposed to wait by the phone, wait for the call back, wait for the agent and the audition. So making is about that direct connection between the audience and the platform [...] We enable them to do whatever they want. Maker typically takes more of a back seat approach. The tools for creation are now in the hands of the individuals. (International Council 2012 NYC: Innovation Without Borders)

In order to achieve this disintermediation and empowerment at scale, Maker studios have, with the Time Warner investment, built an actual studio in Culver City which includes a full-service production studio with facilities that include shooting spaces, production offices, prop and wardrobe areas, editing bays and recording booths. "There is also a creative space, known as the clubhouse, available to members 24 hours a day to hangout and share ideas" (Humphrey 2012). In fact, "Maker is a next-generation, talent-first media company and the only network to offer its partners a full range of vertically integrated services including development, production, promotion, distribution, sales and marketing" (Humphrey 2012). Such structure comes with quasi-corporate frameworks that belie the "We enable them to do whatever they want" mantra:

> When we talk about programming fitting in, it needs to fit in to one of our tent-pole verticals. It needs to add value to what we're already doing, it's less we'll take random things. The point is to focus on broad verticals and then we might go more niche within those verticals, but we do have these key tent-poles that we're focused on. (International Council 2012 NYC: Innovation Without Borders)

DOI: 10.1057/9781137326454

The company recently expanded its multi-vertical approach, and now focuses on comedy, music, gaming, beauty/fashion and Mom's programming both domestically and internationally, especially in Europe.

WIGS – where it gets ... (spicy, interesting, funny, etc) is a high-gloss drama geared toward women that aims for HBO quality and features the contributions of several A- and B-list actors, writers and directors. The ability to attract big names at minimal cost is a clear sign of the ability of the leading new players to challenge the cost structure of premium TV programming, the idea being that "when you get one or two big-name actors, it's a snowball effect" (Acuna 2012). It is one of many examples of going back to the future, with partner/sponsors Unilever, American Express and News Corp (Acuna 2012) evoking 1950s retro TV sponsorship-as-funding arrangements. What isn't retro is the plan to produce daily and weekly content catered according to user comments, with instant feedback to shape the next content delivery (the mantra is "No rules, no ratings guidelines, no boundaries"). WIGS targets a core broadcast demographic, women aged 18 to 49.

YouTube has begun to platform a significant range of *news programming and "fifth estate"* (Dutton 2009) *journalism*. Town Square is youth-oriented news and current affairs produced by The Young Turks. The Young Turks network was the 9th highest earning YouTube partner in 2010, achieving $US112,000 for the year (Wei 2010). A political news and commentary channel seemingly free of corporate media influence, it includes "The Point" (youtube.com/thepoint), a weekly panel discussion show that tackles subjects that are claimed to be regarded as taboo for broadcast television. Other examples of fifth estate journalism include The I-files (youtube.com/ifiles), a partnership between YouTube, the Center for Investigative Reporting, and the Knight Foundation. Truthloader (youtube.com/user/truthloader) is a daily YouTube show bringing investigative and citizen journalism together.

Witness ("See it. Film it. Change it.") was founded in 1992 by Peter Gabriel, attorney Michael Posner and Lawyers Committee for Human Rights (itself formed after the 1991 Rodney King beating). In 2012 Witness partnered with YouTube and Storyful to launch the *Human Rights channel* (youtube.com/humanrights). One of the strengths of "Witness" is its ability to authenticate stories. "Citizen video is increasingly the best and only evidence of serious crimes, yet there does not exist a protocol for authenticating it" (Bair 2012). Witness' partnership with Storyful enables them to investigate the authenticity of each video prior to posting. A

DOI: 10.1057/9781137326454

Witness blog post dated 20 December 2012 (Bair 2012) tells of amateur video that circulated via the online *Syrian Observatory for Human Rights* organisation (syriahr.com) that depicted the atrocities of the ongoing conflict. In order to verify the video, Storyful staff compared the video to a live stream service showing the same event in the same place from a distance. A satellite image of the alleged location depicted the buildings that appear in the video, and 10 other videos from several other sources where later uploaded, further verifying the account. Witness is acutely aware that such verification may not be enough for admissibility in a criminal trial, yet such a rigorous verification process must certainly help advance the use of digital media as evidence in legal hearings.

YouTube has also launched "Next Cause" – a tool that will allow not-for-profits to promote their efforts and obtain one-on-one consulting and community engagement tips to grow their following. A YouTube blog post on 17 February 2012 states: "With 4 billion views a day, we want to make sure nonprofits have the tools they need to reach the global audience on YouTube and turn video views into donations, volunteerism and awareness." The Next Cause program is open to all not for profit organisations that are currently part of the YouTube Nonprofit Program.

The *YouTube Do Gooder* awards are an awards category open to not-for-profits who are part of (or have applied for) the YouTube for Nonprofits program. Sponsored by CISCO, winning entries are highlighted on the YouTube home page for one day. The YouTube Nonprofit Program offers not for profits: "channel branding" (custom thumbnails, logo avatars, backgrounds consistent with organisations branding and public image); "donate buttons" can be placed alongside videos (allowing users to contribute without leaving YouTube site); "live streaming" of galas, fundraisers, conferences etc.; "overlays" – call to action messages (and links) on screen while the videos are playing; "video annotations" provide additional commentary or drive traffic to websites; "community forum" connects non-profits with other non-profits.

There are literally thousands of *education* channels on YouTube now. Universities have a strong presence. (Significant independent initiatives such as the Khan Academy (khanacademy.org), a non-profit educational organisation created by Salman Khan, a graduate of MIT and Harvard Business School, whose mission is to "provide a high quality education for anyone, anywhere" are not discussed here as they are not part of YouTube original channels.) There are a lot of popularising

DOI: 10.1057/9781137326454

channels – science, math, history in particular – that gamify the subject with cool hosts and fun experiments. Numberphile (youtube.com/numberphile) – a YouTube original channel initiative – does things like solving the mathematical route needed to navigate a "choose your own adventure" book successfully. Smart Girls at the Party (smartgirlsattheparty.com and youtube.com/user/smartgirls) is a magazine channel, with a strong educational ("school of life") focus.

Other major platforms

Most commissioned content from the other major platforms are available exclusively on those platforms. Yahoo!'s YouTube channel offers a limited number of clips and advertisements for Yahoo! content that remains available only on Yahoo! An exception to this is Crackle (Sony) which has made all content (including feature length movies) available at crackle.com also available via their YouTube channel. Sony/Crackle has in short skit format *Comedians in Cars Getting Coffee*, with Jerry Seinfeld driving classic cars, visiting a range of cafes/restaurants and hosting various comedians. Yahoo! has concentrated on the same now familiar online format with titles such as *7 Minutes in Heaven, Burning Love, Butterfinger Barmageddon News Network, First Dates with Toby Harris, Hackerazzi, Odd News, Sketchy, Suit Up.* But it also has *Electric City*, Tom Hanks' animated post-apocalyptic web series.

The most significant and widely publicised foray into premium commissioned content was that of Netflix: *Lilyhammer, Arrested Development* (Season 4), *Hemlock Grove* (Gaumont), *House of Cards, Orange is the New Black* (Lionsgate) have been produced for a Netflix first release prior to wider distribution in other release windows in some cases.

House of Cards, starring Kevin Spacey, and developed by Kevin Spacey and Hollywood A-list director David Fincher (*Se7en, Fight Club, The Social Network, The Girl with the Dragon Tattoo*) and playwright Beau Willimon, is based on a BBC miniseries of the same name. Netflix outbid AMC and HBO to secure the series. All episodes were released simultaneously on Netflix and there is evidence that such a premium content strategy is bolstering its brand identity as a quasi-network. According to a survey by Cowen and Co. in February 2103, 86 per cent of Netflix subscribers said having the access to House of Cards makes them less likely to cancel their subscriptions (Roller 2013). *Arrested Development* is a cult favourite

DOI: 10.1057/9781137326454

cancelled in 2006 after three seasons on Fox. After much speculation from fans about possible movies and/or new seasons, the fourth season will premiere on Netflix in May 2013. Like *House of Cards*, all episodes of *Arrested Development will* be released simultaneously. Netflix bested Showtime and Hulu in landing the deal, which includes DVD delivery and video streaming service.

Conclusions

This book has used online screen distribution as a case study of how to research *change* in fast-moving new media phenomena without analytical foreclosure on programmatic optimism or determined scepticism over the potential of new technologies. By definition, the conclusions reached must be provisional – in the spirit of Elizabeth Eisenstein (1979), we must seek to understand the "transitional times" without recourse to totalising explanatory schema, or, with Thomas Streeter, to measure significance by "[its] productivity, by the ways in which [it has] made a difference" (in Lee and Streeter 2012).

Although the rate of change in the online screen distribution of film and television has been modest over the past decade, the pace is now accelerating. When compared to the impact of P2P on the music industry, and the blogosphere and online classified advertising on newspapers and journalism, change in film and television has been slower and has had less disruptive influence – to this point. Rates of change in book publishing and magazines have been somewhat slower than in film. These comparisons would seem to some extent logical given the nature of the content in each category.

Key issues faced by online distribution pioneers from 1997 to the mid 2000s included the lack of a quality viewing experience – online distribution of rich video requires high speed broadband which is only recently beginning to diffuse globally. Combined with primitive video compression compared to today's standards, it meant that movies took many hours or even days to download over a dial-up connection and very few websites offered a wide selection of box office hits. Movies available as paid downloads online were mostly B product. In addition, until large panel LCD screens for computers and large panel plasma, LCD and LED TVs diffused widely amongst the consumer base from the mid-2000s onwards. Watching movies or TV shows on a small computer screen

DOI: 10.1057/9781137326454

before that time was not, to say the least, an optimal viewing experience. However, the prime mover, arguably, was Hollywood's slowing rather than hastening change.

Of course, downloading for free was burgeoning throughout this period via reasonably efficient but also sophisticated platforms such as BitTorrent. The majors spent the best part of the 15-year period we are canvassing (a period of experimentation and innovation) putting energy into denial, threat and attempted litigation (and megaphone diplomacy directed at east Asia when most download piracy is estimated to occur inside the US) while pirated downloading continued to create viable work-arounds and a parallel culture of consumption with its own "innovation" champions.

But, as we have argued, there were strong indicators from 2008 onward to confirm that online distribution may be following the classic four-stage industry lifecycle. Recent developments would indicate that it has now moved from the initial fragmentation stage where industry structures were evolving, barriers to entry were low and new firms proliferated in search of customers, into the shakeout stage where market growth escalates, industry structures consolidate and dominant players emerge through organic growth or via mergers and acquisitions and many enterprises fail (including Veoh, Joost, BSide, Dovetail, Caachi, and Zoie).

It has been the central theme of the book that there are some genuinely new players in online distribution of film and TV that are challenging the dominance of traditional players, and there has been an intense rehearsal of mostly established but also some new business models, like micropayments, which principally are based around what we have called the IT-innovation model. It is a central argument of the book that the Majors have an ownership stake in only one of these new players, Hulu (Sony's Crackle does not operate on the same scale as Hulu) – and we have suggested its ownership structure and strategy is not stable.

The fundamental difference between the third wave of market leaders such as Apple/iTunes, Amazon, Yahoo!, Facebook and YouTube and the previous waves – one which optimises their chances of being able to formulate successful business models and better monetise screen content online – is that they were Internet pure-play companies that already had or have been able to develop a critical mass of online customers and possessed extensive data on their past online search behaviour and purchasing habits. In addition, they had years of experience marketing directly

DOI: 10.1057/9781137326454

to their customer base targeting those most likely to be interested in a particular genre or program based on web analytics of each individual's past behaviour and any product feedback that they may have provided. The fact they have been prepared to work around content blocking tactics of the Majors by commissioning new content is to observe not only history repeating itself but also substantial change in the modes of presentation and distribution of content.

Apple, in transmogrifying from a computer manufacturer to an integrator of devices, platform, portals and content and so a dominant player in online distribution of music, movie and TV shows, exemplified the "IT-innovation" model. It has included selling what the content industry calls premium content at price-points below the latter's acceptability threshold in order principally to sell devices – iPod, iPhone, Apple TV – at premium prices. This has accelerated the long-term movement from premium product to curated services in the audio-visual environment. The Hollywood studios were likely forced, by the entry of iTunes into the paid download market, to abandon their initial approaches (Movielink and Moviebeam) and are now experimenting with Hulu (streaming advertising supported content) and Hulu Plus (an SVOD service on a mixed subscription/ad supported model) to create a sustainable business, more along the lines of Pay TV.

The rapid success of iTunes must be emphasised: since it began offering movies and TV shows as paid downloads in 2006, it has dominated the paid-for online video download market and was selling 50,000 movies globally daily in 2008 (Screen Digest 2008). The die had thus been cast. This was a significant disruption to standard business models because it sold premium or near-premium content at close to break-even with a view to profit from hardware device sales and to "buy" market share. This was an anathema to Hollywood's notion of the value of premium content and gave rise to the normative concern, shared widely amongst the established media industries, that the current choice is "analogue dollars" or "digital cents". Having said that, it is also acknowledged that Hollywood has also pressured Apple over time, to raise prices – and price-points for movie and TV programs sales on iTunes have slowly increased. Against the assumption that open systems are normatively more progressive, Apple's closed "ecology" solved, at least in principle, the micropayment conundrum and opened up a potentially sustainable, relatively disintermediated, revenue stream for content creators.

DOI: 10.1057/9781137326454

There is also a blurring of the boundaries between amateur and professional content, and some shift on the new platforms between US and ROW content sources. Several of YouTube's originals channels have been commissioned from those who were amateurs coming through the YouTube Partnership program. The degree to which the independent sector and UGC could be integrated into an innovative distribution model is visible in the case of Amazon. That promise may be realised if the online distribution platforms provided by Amazon via its subsidiaries (Amazon Studios and CreateSpace placing original content on Amazon Instant Video and LoveFilm, and enabling producers to leverage Withoutabox to market their content, together with imdb.com to build their industry profiles) are successfully exploited. Nevertheless, the formidable difference in scale and investment between mainstream online distribution and those which seek to service independent and ROW cinema reminds us of the bounded nature of this current disruption to Hollywood's established practices.

Similar conclusions may be reached from our sampling of the new, commissioned content earlier in this chapter. It should be remembered that, until this commissioning phase, licit online content was more mainstream and less diverse than that which existed in cable, satellite and DVD niche retail in most major territories. Clearly, the material we have surveyed represents a varying degree of innovation in terms of mode of distribution, style and range of providers but there is much experimentation with a wide range of original content, a level of "off-Broadway" professional, pro–am and tyro experimentation not typically seen before in the professional TV space.

Does it matter? New, powerful players have entered the market, some of whom massively outrank in size and growth the companies which run film and television today. Like all large-scale corporations, they are likely to use market power to seek to limit competition and most will attempt to corral users inside walled gardens. But, through them, distribution of licit screen content has never before been so varied and accessible. They have provided platforms and implemented strategies that have seen some new types of pro–am and professional content come to the fore. They are beginning to invest directly in content whereas hitherto it was mostly a case of aggregating others' content. Commissioned content providers come from a wide range of countries. Overall, we would argue that all that matters.

DOI: 10.1057/9781137326454

References

Acuna, Kirsten. 2012. "First look: Wigs – the YouTube channel that will change the way we watch TV." *Business Insider*, 5 May. Accessed 12 February 2013 http://www.businessinsider.com/youtube-wigs-channel-2012-5?op=1#ixzz2LxJvOPya

Agence France Press. 2007. "Independent film makers win online stage." *The Age*, 29 October. Accessed 14 June 2011 http://news.theage.com.au/technology /independent-film-makers-win-Online -stage-20071029–16rz.html

Alexa.com. 2012. "MUBI." Accessed 19 February 2013 http://www.alexa.com/siteinfo/mubi.com

Amazon Studios. 2012. "About the Amazon Studios development process." *Amazon Studios Frequently Asked Questions*. Accessed 16 February 2013 http://studios.amazon.com/getting-started#peoples_production

Anderson, Chris. 2012. *Makers: the new industrial revolution.* New York: Random House Business.

Andrews, Robert. 2009. "Interview: Mike Volpi: Broadcasters' own VOD plans killed Joost." *Paid content.com*, 6 July 6. Accessed 14 June 2011 http://paidcontent.co.uk/article/419-interview-mike-volpi-broadcasters-own-vod-plans-killed-Joost/

AsiaMediaJournal. 2012. "Baidu buys Providence iQiYi shares." *Asia media journal*, 2 November. Accessed 2 November 2012 http://www.asiamediajournal.com /pressrelease.php?id=4259

Bair, Madeleine. 2012. "Is it authentic? When citizens and soldiers document war." *Witness Blog*, 20 November.

DOI: 10.1057/9781137326454

Accessed 8 December 2012 http://blog.witness.org/2012/11/is-it-authentic-when-citizens-and-soldiers-document-war/

Baldwin, Drew. 2012a. "YouTube's 'Next Cause' program gives nonprofits a huge boost." *Tubefilter News*, 21 February. Accessed 16 February 2013 http://www.tubefilter.com/2012/02/21/youtube-next-cause/

Baldwin, Drew. 2012b. "iJustine jumpstarts YouTube Next Vlogger program." *Tubefilter News*, 31 March. Accessed 16 February 2013 http://www.tubefilter.com/2012/03/31/youtube-next-vlogger-ijustine/

Baldwin, Drew. 2012c. "Hulu and Warner Brothers to debut original series from 'Sex and the City' writer." *Tubefilter News*, 7 February. Accessed 7 February 2012 http://www.tubefilter.com/2012/02/07/hulu-and-warner-bros-to-debut-original-series-from-sex-and-the-city-writer/

Balio, Tino, ed. 1985. *The American film industry*. Wisconsin and London: The University of Wisconsin Press Madison.

Barr, Trevor. 2011. "Television's newcomers: Netflix, Apple, Google and Facebook." *Telecommunications Journal of Australia* 6 (4): 60.1–60.10

Baxter, Richard. 2009. "Video market monitor: India." *Screen Digest*, September. Accessed 14 June 2011 http://www.screendigest.com/reports/09videomarketmonitorindia/pdf/SD-09-09-VideoMarketMonitorIndia/view.html

Belloni, Matthew. 2012. "Les Moonves: Steve Jobs approached CBS for Apple TV content." *Hollywood Reporter*, 10 March. Accessed 10 March 2012 http://www.hollywoodreporter.com/news/leslie-moonves-steve-jobs-cbs-apple-tv-298300

Bennett, James and Strange, Niki. 2011. *Television as digital media*. Durham: Duke University Press.

Binazewski, Peter. 2011. "Warner Brothers Entertainment becomes first Hollywood studio to launch a 'social series' on Facebook." *Time Warner Press Release from Warner Brothers Digital Distribution*, 29 September. Accessed 16 February 2013 http://www.timewarner.com/newsroom/press-releases/2011/09/Warner_Bros_Entertainment_Becomes_First_Hollywood_Studio_09–29–2011.php

BizShark. 2011. "Jaman.com/traffic". Accessed 4 April 2011 http://www.bizshark.com/company/jaman.com/traffic

Blumenthal, Howard J. and Goodenough, Oliver R. 2006. *This business of television: a standard guide to the television industry*. 3rd edn. New York: Billboard Books.

Bordwell, David and Noël Carroll, eds. 1996. *Post-Theory: reconstructing film studies*. Madison: University of Wisconsin Press.

DOI: 10.1057/9781137326454

Bricklin, Julia. 2012. "Original programming is the right direction for Netflix." *Forbes,* 30 April. Accessed 30 April 2012 http://www.forbes.com/sites/juliabricklin/2012/04/30/original-programming-is-right-direction-for-netflix/

Broughton, Richard. 2009. "Video-on-demand yet to develop." *Screen Digest,* January 13–20.

Brown, Les. 1977. *The New York Times encyclopaedia of television.* Toronto: Times Books.

Bulkley, Kate. 2007. "What exactly is Bebo's business model?" *Broadcast,* 21 November. Accessed 17 January 2012 http://www.broadcastnow.co.uk/news/multi-platform/comment/what-exactly-is-bebos-business-model/294114.article

Bulkley, Kate. 2012. "MIPTV 2012: Lionsgate's 'End Game' close to getting second run." *Hollywood Reporter,* 4 April. Accessed 4 April 2012 http://www.hollywoodreporter.com/news/miptv-2012-lionsgatess-end-game-308166

Businessweek. 2011. "QiYi.com, Inc. to invest CNY 200 million in self-made content in 2012." *Businessweek,* 25 November. Accessed 25 November 2011 http://investing.businessweek.com/research/stocks/private/snapshot.asp?privcapId=98904258

Business Wire. 2007. "Joost closes $45 million in financing." *Business Wire,* 10 May. Accessed 14 June 2011 http://www.businesswire.com/portal/site/home/permalink/?ndmViewId=news_view&newsId=20070509006451&newsLang=en

Butcher, Mark. 2011. "Film site MUBI pulls in $2.4 million to socialise cinema buffs." *Techcrunch,* 7 January. Accessed 20 February 2013 http://techcrunch.com/2011/01/07/film-site-mubi-pulls-in-2-4-million-to-socialise-cinema-buffs/

Carlson, Richard. 2011. "The bidding war over Hulu erupts – find out who's in and who's out." *Business Insider,* 31 August. Accessed 16 February 2013 http://articles.businessinsider.com/2011-08-31/tech/30128648_1_hulu-ceo-jason-kilar-amazon-prime-larry-page

Cavernelis, Dennis. 2008. "Studio breaks rules to fight online piracy." *Los Angeles Times,* 11 November. Accessed 1 November 2008 http://articles.latimes.com/2008/nov/04/business/fi-warner4

Chandra, Rishi. 2010. "Google 1/0: Google TV keynote: Introducing google TV." Accessed 16 February 2013 http://www.youtube.com/watch?v=ASZbArr7vdI

DOI: 10.1057/9781137326454

China Daily. 2012. "Youku contest attracts millions." *China Daily,* 5 June. Accessed 8 August 2012 http://www.chinadaily.com.cn/entertainment/2012–06/05/content_15474569.htm

Chmielewski, Dawn C. and Guynn, Jessica. 2010. "Google TV plan is causing jitters in Hollywood." *Los Angeles Times,* 17 August. Accessed 16 February 2013 http://articles.latimes.com/2010/aug/17/business/la-fi-ct-googletv-20100818

Chosick, Amy and Stelter, Brian. 2012. "An online TV site grows up." *New York Times,* 16 April. Accessed 16 April 2012 http://www.nytimes.com/2012/04/17/business/media/hulu-the-online-tv-site-adds-original-programming.html?pagewanted=all

Christensen, Clayton M. 1997. *The innovator's dilemma: when new technologies cause great firms to fail.* Boston: Harvard Business School Press.

Christian, Amyar Jean. 2012a. "Beyond big video: the instability of independent networks in a new media market." *Continuum: Journal of Media & Cultural Studies* 26 (1): 73–87.

Christian, Amyar Jean. 2012b. "The web as television reimagined? Online networks and the pursuit of legacy media." *Journal of Communication Inquiry* 36 (4): 340–56.

Chua, Beng-Huat. 2012. *Structure, audience and soft power in East Asian pop culture.* Hong Kong: Hong Kong University Press.

Cineuropa. 2010. "Video on demand distribution in Europe – Case study: Movieurope.com. Interview with Niels Albaek Jensen, Founder & Managing Director, FIDD." *Cineuropa,* 19 July. Accessed 14 June 2011 http://cineuropa.org/dossier.aspx?lang=en&treeID=1308&documentID=148726

Cineuropa. 2011. "MUBI signs slew of deals." *Cineuropa,* 12 May. Accessed 19 February 2013 http://cineuropa.org/nw.aspx?t=newsdetail&l=en&did=203465

Cohen, Joshua. 2011. "Introducing YouTube's next Emeril Lagasse, Tara Stiles." *Tubefilter News,* 10 November. Accessed 16 February 2013 http://www.tubefilter.com/2011/11/10/youtube-next-chef-trainer/

Cohen, Joshua. 2012a. "My Damn Channel to do it LIVE on YouTube." *Tubefilter News,* 21 March. Accessed 16 February 2013 http://www.tubefilter.com/2012/03/21/my-damn-channel-live-youtube/

DOI: 10.1057/9781137326454

Cohen, Joshua. 2012b. "What's next for YouTube Next?" *Tubefilter News*, 7 February. Accessed 16 February 2013 http://www.tubefilter.com/2012/02/07/whats-next-for-youtube-next/

Cohen, Joshua. 2012c. "Yahoo's video viewership boost, edges out Vevo." *Mashable*, 20 March. Accessed 20 March 2012 http://mashable.com/2012/03/20/yahoo-video-views/

Cohen, Joshua. 2012d. "Hulu spends the first of its $500 million on original programs?" *Tubefilter News*, 16 January. Accessed 16 January 2012 http://www.tubefilter.com/2012/01/16/hulu-battleground/

Cohen, Joshua. 2012e. "Maker Studios gets one billion views ... a month." *Tubefilter*, 30 June. Accessed 25 February 2013 *http://www.tubefilter.com/2012/06/30/maker-studios-billion-views/*

comScore. 2009. "Americans viewed a record 16.8 billion videos online in April driven largely by surge in viewership on YouTube." *comScore VideoMetrix*, 4 June. Accessed 18 February 2013 http://ir.comscore.com/releasedetail.cfm?ReleaseID=388126

comScore. 2012. "comScore releases October 2012 U.S. online video rankings." *comScore*, 15 November. Accessed 16 February 2013 http://www.comscore.com/Insights/Press_Releases/2012/11/comScore_Releases_October_2012_U.S._Online_Video_Rankings

Curran, James, Fenton, Natalie, and Freedman, Des. 2012. *Misunderstanding the Internet*. London and New York: Routledge.

Curtin, Michael. 2003. "Media capital: towards the study of spatial flows." *International Journal of Cultural Studies* 6 (2): 202–228.

Curtin, Michael. 2007. *Playing to the World's biggest audience: the globalization of Chinese film and TV*. Los Angeles: University of California Press.

Davis, Noah. 2011. "Google has big ass ideas for Hulu and it's willing to spend billions more than anyone else to get it." *Business Insider*, 6 April. Accessed 16 February 2013 http://www.businessinsider.com/google-buy-hulu-2011-9

Dawtrey, Adam. 2011. "Warner Bros. pacts with Lovefilm in U.K." *Variety*, 17 November. Accessed 17 November 2012 http://www.variety.com/article/VR1118046266

Dutton, William H. 2009. "The fifth estate emerging through the network of networks." *Prometheus* 27 (1): 1–15.

Edwards, Cliff. 2012. "Microsoft skips cinemas with $10 million Halo film on YouTube." *The Sydney Morning Herald, Digital Life*, 5 October. Accessed 6 October 2012. http://www.smh.com.au/digital-life/games/

DOI: 10.1057/9781137326454

microsoft-skips-cinemas-with-10-million-halo-film-on-youtube-
20121005–2736i.html

Edwards, Cliff and Yablon, Alexander. 2012. "Netflix reaches deal
to stream Weinstein Co.'s 'The Artist.'" *Bloomberg Business Week,*
22 February. Accessed 22 February 2012 http://www.businessweek.
com/news/2012–02–22/netflix-reaches-deal-to-stream-weinstein-
co-s-the-artist-.html

Efrati, Amir and Schuker, Lauren A. E. 2011. "YouTube tees up big
talent." *Wall Street Journal,* 29 October. Accessed 16 February 2013
http://online.wsj.com/article/SB100014240529702036875045770041702
00345732.html

Eisenstein, Elizabeth, 2 vols. ed. 1979. *The printing press as an agent of
change: communications and cultural transformations in early modern
Europe.* Cambridge: Cambridge University Press.

Elgin, Ben. 2006. "Yahoo's boulevard of broken dreams." *Bloomberg
Business Week,* 13 March. Accessed 16 February 2013 http://www.
businessweek.com/magazine/content/06_11/b3975097.htm

Eller, Claudia and Miller, Greg. 2000. "Pop.com, IFilm break off merger
talks." *Los Angeles Times,* 2 September. Accessed 18 February 2013
http://articles.latimes.com/2000/sep/02/business/fi-14353

Fingas, Jon. 2012. "Baidu buys control of streaming media portal iQiyi,
raises stakes in China's media wars." *Endgadget.com,* 4 November.
Accessed 25 February 2013 http://www.engadget.com/2012/11/04
/baidu-buys-control-of-streaming-video-portal-iqiyi/

Fixmer, Andy and Satariano, Adam. 2011. "Apple is said to be
considering bidding for Hulu online TV service." *Bloomberg News,*
23 July. Accessed 16 February 2013 http://www.bloomberg.com/
news/2011–07–21/apple-said-to-consider-making-an-offer-for-hulu-
online-television-service.html

Flint, Joe. 2011. "Netflix to bring back Arrested Development." *Los
Angeles Times,* 18 November. Accessed 16 February 2013 http://
latimesblogs.latimes.com/entertainmentnewsbuzz/2011/11/netflix-to-
bring-back-arrested-development.html

Frankel, Daniel. 2012. "Hulu's growing up, but what about its parents?"
Yahoo! Finance, 17 April. Accessed 17 April, 2012 http://finance.yahoo.
com/news/hulu-growing-parents-211352301.html

Fritz, Ben. 2012. "Netflix to premiere all eight episodes of 'Lilyhammer'
simultaneously." *Los Angeles Times,* 3 January. Accessed 3 January 2012
http://latimesblogs.latimes.com/entertainmentnewsbuzz/2012/01/

DOI: 10.1057/9781137326454

netflix-to-premiere-all-eight-episodes-of-lilyhammer-simutaneously.
html

Gannes, Liz. 2009. "YouTube changes everything: the online video
revolution." In *Television goes digital*, edited by Darcy Gerbarg,
147–155. New York: Springer.

Garrahan, Mike. 2012. "GE squares up to Apple in iTunes case."
Financial Times FT.com, 23 May. Accessed 23 May 2012 http://
www.ft.com/cms/s/0/5f34ca8c-a4ec-11e1-b421–00144feabdc0.
html#axzz2Kpmhm7Pa

Gerbarg, Darcy, ed. 2009. *Television goes digital*. New York: Springer.

Goldberg, Lesley. 2012. " 'CSI' creator Anthony Zuiker sets
'Cybergeddon' for Yahoo!" *Hollywood Reporter*, 20 March. Accessed
20 March 2012 http://www.hollywoodreporter.com/live-feed/csi-
anthony-zuiker-yahoo-cybergeddon-302452

Gomery, Douglas. 1985. "The coming of television and the 'Lost' motion
picture audience." *Journal of Film and Video* 37 (3): 5–11.

Google. 2013. "About Google." Accessed 16 February 2013. http://www.
google.com/about

Graham, Jefferson. 2002. "Studios aim to squash movie piracy." *USA
Today*, 11 November. Accessed 14 June 2011 http://www.usatoday.com/
life/movies/news/2002–11–11-movielink_x.htm

Graser, Marc. 2012. " 'Fistful' of online content: Maker Studios
looks to make mark on YouTube with Western-mashup." *Variety*,
30 July. Accessed 25 February 2013 http://www.variety.com/article/
VR1118057247/

Gray, Jason. 2009. "Warner Bros to speed up VOD releases in Japan."
Screen Daily.com, 28 May. Accessed 18 February 2013 http://www.
screendaily.com/5001913.article

Gray, Jason (2009) "Five Japanese majors join forces for VOD movie
channel." *Screen Daily.com* March 30th, 2009. Accessed online at:
http://www.screendaily.com/five-japanese-majors-join-forces-for-
vod-movie-channel/4043829.article

Greenberg, Tony. 2011. "Jumping through the hoops with Hulu: will
Hollywood studios kill their offspring once again?" *Huffington Post*,
20 September. Accessed 16 February 2013 http://www.huffingtonpost.
com/tony-greenberg/jumping-through-hoops- wit_b_970928.html

Gripsrud, Jostein. 2010. *Relocating television: television in the digital
context*. London: Routledge.

DOI: 10.1057/9781137326454

Grover, Ronald. 2000. "What burst Pop.com's bubble?" *Business Week*, 25 September. Accessed 26 June 2011 http://www.businessweek. com/2000/00_39/b3700102.htm

Groves, Don. 2010. "Amazon goes Hollywood." Accessed 18 February 2013 http://www.sbs.com.au/films/blog-articles/121272/Amazon-goes-Hollywood

Gruenwedel, Erik. 2012a. "IHS: Netflix tops Apple in online movie revenue." *Home Media Magazine*, 1 June. Accessed 20 February 2013 http://www.homemediamagazine.com/netflix/ihs-netflix-tops-apple-online-movie-revenue-27414

Gruenwedel, Erik. 2012b. "Netflix subs streamed 1 billion hours of content in June." *Home Media Magazine*, 3 July. Accessed 3 July 2012 http://www.homemediamagazine.com/netflix/netflix-subs-streamed-1-billion-hours-content-june-27717

Gruenwedel, Erik. 2012c. "Netflix bows service in Sweden." *Home Media Magazine*, 15 October. Accessed 15 October 2012 http://www. homemediamagazine.com/netflix/netflix-bows-service-sweden-28578

Gruenwedel, Erik. 2012d. "Netflix touts 30 million streaming subs." *Home Media Magazine,* 25 October. Accessed 25 October 2012 http:// www.homemediamagazine.com/netflix/netflix-touts-30-million-streaming-subs-28672

Guglielmo, Connie. 2012. "Google invests in Machinima, sees 'financial return'." *Forbes*, 21 May. Accessed 25 February 2013 http://www. forbes.com/sites/connieguglielmo/2012/05/21/google-invests-in-machinima-sees-financial-return/

Gutelle, Sam. 2012a. "YouTube goes international, adds 60 original channels to Initiative." *Tubefilter*, 8 October. Accessed 8 October 2012 http://www.tubefilter.com/2012/10/08/youtube-original-channels-initiative-new-international/

Gutelle, Sam. 2012b. "YouTube introduces ten innovative educators as Next EDU gurus." *Tubefilter*, 17 October. Accessed 17 October 2012 http://www.tubefilter.com/2012/10/17/youtube-next-edu-gurus-winners/

Gutelle, Sam. 2012c. "Hulu now over 3 million paying subscribers; 2012 revenue nears $700m." *Tubefilter.com*, 26 December. Accessed 27 December 2012 http://www.tubefilter.com/2012/12/26/hulu-plus-subscribers-revenue-700-million/

DOI: 10.1057/9781137326454

Gutelle, Sam. 2012d. "Maker Studios: 'Time Warner was the best fit.'" *Tubefilter*, 21 December. Accessed 25 February 2013 http://www. tubefilter.com/2012/12/21/maker-studios-courtney-holt-time-warner-investment-interview/

Guynn, Jessica and Chmielewski, Dawn C. 2011. "Google Inc. in preliminary talks to buy Hulu." *Los Angeles Times*, 1 July. Accessed 21 October 2012 http://latimesblogs.latimes.com/ entertainmentnewsbuzz/2011/06/google-in-preliminary-talks-to-buy-hulu-.html

Habermas, Jürgen. 2006. "Political communication in media society: does democracy still enjoy an epistemic dimension? The impact of normative theory on empirical research". *Communication Theory* 16 (4): 411–426.

Hachman, Mark. 2008. "New Sezmi set top blows away the TV." *PC Mag*, 1 May. Accessed 18 February 2013 http://www.pcmag.com /article2/0,2817,2289653,00.asp

Hale, Mike. 2012. "YouTube dramas aimed at women." *New York Times*, 4 October. Accessed 4 October 2012 http://www.nytimes. com/2012/10/05/arts/television/wigs-channel-on-youtube-aimed-at-women.html

Hampton, Benjamin B. 1970. *History of the American film industry from its beginnings to 1931*. Reprinted from 1931. New York: Dover Publications Inc.

Handke, Christian. 2006. "Plain destruction or creative destruction – copyright erosion and the evolution of the record industry." *Review of Economic Research on Copyright Issues* 3 (2): 29–51.

Horan, Peter C. and Rayport, Jeffrey F. 2011. "Who Rules the Web Now?" *Harvard Business Review*, 22 February. Accessed 5 October 2012 http://blogs.hbr.org/cs/2011/02/who_rules_the_web_now.html

Huettig, Mae D. 1944. *Economic control of the motion picture industry – a study of industrial organization*. Philadelphia: University of Pennsylvania Press.

Humphrey, Michael. 2012. "Maker Studios: the YouTube savants talk channel expansion." Forbes, 7 November. Accessed 25 February 2013 http://www.forbes.com/sites/michaelhumphrey/2011/11/07/maker-studios-the-youtube-savants-talk-channel-expansion/

Hustvedt, Marc. 2011a. "YouTube Next: Google acquires Next New Networks". *Tubefilter News,* 7 March. Accessed 11 February 2012 http://

DOI: 10.1057/9781137326454

www.tubefilter.com/2011/03/07/youtube-next-google-acquires-next-new-networks/

Hustvedt, Marc. 2011b. "Hulu Japan launches, 100% ad-free, 0% web originals." *Tubefilter.com*, 1 September. Accessed 16 February 2013 http://www.tubefilter.com/2011/09/01/hulu-japan/

Ingram, Matthew. 2010. "Yahoo banking on original content – again." *Gigaom*, 2 April. Accessed 16 February 2013 http://gigaom.com/2010/04/02/yahoo-banking-on-original-content-again/

International Council 2012. "Interview with Courtney Holt, COO, Maker Studios." *International Council 2012 NYC: Innovation without borders*, 15 November. Accessed 25 February 2013 http://fora.tv/2012/11/15/courtney_holt_coo_maker_studios

Jobs, Steve. 2010. "AppleTV 2010 – Steve Jobs shakes up the media with new on-demand system Keynote 2010." *YouTube.com*, 4 September. Accessed 16 February 2013 http://www.youtube.com/watch?v=3JZyG1vjeNg

Jowett, Garth and Linton, James. M. 1980. *Movies as mass communication*. Beverly Hills: Sage.

Kafka, Peter. 2012a. "Changing channels: YouTube will pull the plug on at least 60 percent of its programming deals." *AllThingsD.com*, 11 November. Accessed 11 November 2012 http://allthingsd.com/20121111/changing-channels-youtube-starts-renewing-some-but-not-all-of-its-programming-deals/

Kafka, Peter. 2012b. "YouTube's gigantic year is already here, Citi says." *AllThingsD.com*, 21 June. Accessed 21 June 2012 http://allthingsd.com/20120621/youtubes-gigantic-year-is-already-here-citi-says/

Kafka, Peter. 2012c. "Amazon gets into the sitcom business." *AllThingsD.com*, 2 May. Accessed 2 May 2012 http://allthingsd.com/20120502/amazon-gets-into-the-sitcom-business/

Kain, E.D. 2012. "Could the new Netflix Exclusive series 'Lilyhammer' give new life to online television?" *Forbes.com*, 3 January. Accessed 3 January 2012 http://www.forbes.com/sites/erikkain/2012/01/03/could-the-new-netflix-exclusive-series-lilyhammer-breath-new-life-into-online-television/

Keane, Michael. 2013. *Creative industries in China: art, design, media*. London: Polity.

Kindem, Goram, ed. 1982. *The American movie industry*. Carbondale: Southern Illinois University Press.

DOI: 10.1057/9781137326454

Knee, Jonathan A. "Why content isn't king". *Atlantic Monthly*. July/
    August 2011. Accessed 27 October 2012. http://www.theatlantic.com/
    magazine/archive/2011/07/why-content-isn-8217-t-king/8551/
Kryncl, Robert. 2012. "YouTube original channels go global".
    Broadcasting Ourselves. The Official YouTube Blog, 7 October. Accessed
    7 October 2012 http://youtube-global.blogspot.com.au/2012/10/
    youtubes-original-channels-go-global.html
Landa, Chris. 2012. "The increasingly blurry line between TV and
    online originals." *Tubefilter.com*, 14 March. Accessed 14 March 2012
    http://www.tubefilter.com/2012/03/14/hulu-originals-tv/
Landreth, Jonathan. 2008. "Warners sets VOD in China." *Hollywood
    Reporter*, 5 November. Accessed 14 June 2011 http://www.
    allbusiness.com/media-telecommunications/movies-sound-
    recording/11689404–1.html
Lange, Andre. 2009. "A first census of audiovisual on-demand services
    in Europe." *Observing audiovisual on-demand services in the European
    Union: market and regulatory issues*, Brussels, 3 November. Accessed
    14 June 2011 http://ec.europa.eu/avpolicy/docs/other_actions/eao/
    census.pdf
Lanham, Richard A. 2006. *The economics of attention: style and substance
    in the age of information*. Chicago: University of Chicago Press.
Lash, Scott and Urry, John. 1987. *The end of organised capital*. Madison:
    University of Wisconsin Press
Lawler, Ryan. 2012. "YouTube shows Silicon Valley how it can beat
    Hollywood". *Gigaom.com*, 23 January. Accessed 23 January 2012 http://
    gigaom.com/video/youtube-beats-hollywood/
Learmonth, Michael. 2011. "YouTube's new sell: want to buy a web
    series for $3.5 million?" *Advertising Age*, 14 July. Accessed 16 February
    2013 http://adage.com/article/digital/youtube-s-sell-buy-a-web-
    series/228712/
Lee, Chin-Chuan. 1979. *Media imperialism reconsidered: the homogenizing
    of television culture*. Beverly Hills: Sage Publications.
Lee, Hye Jin and Streeter, Thomas. 2012. "Romancing the Internet: an
    interview with Thomas Streeter". *Journal of Communication Inquiry*
    36 (2): 95–110.
Leffler, Rebecca. 2007. "French VOD Site UniversCine going live."
    Hollywood Reporter, 18 April. Accessed 14 June 2011 http://www.
    hollywoodreporter.com/news/french-vod-site-universcine-going-
    134335

DOI: 10.1057/9781137326454

Leverette, Marc, Ott, Brian L., and Buckley, Cara Louise. 2008. *It's not TV: watching HBO in the post-television era.* New York: Routledge.

Levin, Jordan. 2009. "An industry perspective: calibrating the velocity of change." In *Media industries: history, theory and method,* edited by Jennifer Holt and Alisa Perren, 256–263. Malden: Wiley-Blackwell.

Levy, Stephen. 2011. "Jeff Bezos owns the Web in more ways than you think." *Wired.com,* 13 November. Accessed 13 February 2013 http://www.wired.com/magazine/2011/11/ff_bezos/all/

Lewis, Howard T. 1933. *The motion picture industry.* New York: D. Van Nostrand Co. Inc.

Lieberman, Al. and Esgate, Patricia. 2002. *The entertainment marketing revolution.* Upper Saddle River, NJ; London. Financial Times Prentice Hall.

Lobato, Ramon. 2009. "The politics of digital distribution: exclusionary structures in online cinema." *Studies in Australasian Cinema* 3 (2): 167–178.

Loeffler, Tania. 2010. "Online film spending near doubled." *Screen Digest,* April, 105. Accessed 2 September 2011 http://www.screendigest.com/reports/100421c/10_04_Online _film_spending_near_doubled/view.html

Lotz, Amanda. 2007. *The television will be revolutionized.* New York: New York University Press.

Luo, Benny. 2012. "Maker Studios beats Macinima – Now ranked the #1 independent YouTube network on comScore." *New Media Rockstars,* 19 October. Accessed 25 February 2013 http://newmediarockstars.com/2012/10/maker-studios-surpasses-machinima/

Manarino, Matthew. 2012. "Maker Studios: 1 billion YouTube views in one month." *New Media Rockstars,* 30 June. Accessed 25 February 2013 http://newmediarockstars.com/2012/06/maker-studios-hits-1-billion-youtube-views-in-one-month-exclusive/

Manjoo, Farhad. 2009. "Do you think bandwidth grows on trees?" *Slate Technology,* 14 April. Accessed 18 February 2013 http://www.slate.com/articles/technology/technology/2009/04/do_you_think_bandwidth_grows_on_trees.html

Marshall, Matt. 2011. "With Google TV channels on YouTube, it's time to chuck cable." *Venture Beat.com,* 31 October. Accessed 16 February 2013 http://venturebeat.com/2011/10/31/with-google's-tv-channels-on-youtube-its-time-to-consider-chucking-cable-tv/

DOI: 10.1057/9781137326454

Marx, W. David and Gould, Matthew. 2010. "YouTube in Japan to offer MLB.jp channel featuring full-length games and highlights of Major League Baseball." *YouTube and MLB.jp*, 30 August. Accessed 16 February 2013 http://mlb.mlb.com/mlb/international/downloads/yt-mlb_pr_english_1220.pdf

McDonald, Andrew. 2011. "Google TV heading for Europe." *C21Media*, 26 August. Accessed 16 February 2013 http://www.c21media.net/archives/55659

McGahan, Anita M., Argyres, Nicholas and Baum, Joel A.C. 2004. "Context, technology and strategy: forging new perspectives on the industry lifecycle". In *Business strategy over the industry lifecycle (Advances in Strategic Management, Volume 21)*, edited by Joel A.C. Baum and Anita M. McGahan, 1–21. Bingley, UK: Emerald Group Publishing.

Miller, Liz Shannon. 2011. "Is Facebook the way to go for new originals." *Gigaom.com*, 23 October. Accessed 16 February 2013 http://gigaom.com/video/facebook-web-originals/

Miller, Toby. 2010. *Television: the basics*. Abingdon: Routledge.

Morrison, Scott. 2011. "Google buys web video start-up Next New Networks to help YouTube video creators." *The Australian*, 8 March. Accessed 16 February 2013 http://www.theaustralian.com.au/business/world/google-buys-web-video-start-up-next-new-networks-to-help-youtube-video-creators/story-e6frg900-1226017628971

MUBI. 2012. "Partners." Accessed 19 February 2013 http://MUBI.com/about/partners

Murphy, Claire. 2008. "Drama that's ahead of the pack." *The Guardian*, 22 September. Accessed 8 December 2009 http://www.guardian.co.uk/changingadvertising/web.productions

Netflix. 2012. "Company facts: Netflix is the world's leading Internet subscription service for enjoying movies and TV shows." *Netflix.com*. Accessed 29 November, 2012 https://signup.netflix.com/MediaCenter/Facts

Nielsen. 2009. "Middle agers help Hulu grow 490%" *Nielsen Online*, 18 May. Accessed 19 May, 2009 http://www.marketingcharts.com/television/middle-agers-help-hulu-grow-490-9125/

Noam, Eli. 2010. "Hollywood 2.0: how Internet distribution will affect the film industry." In *Media, technology and society*, edited by W. Russell Neuman, 59–69. Ann Arbor: University of Michigan Press.

DOI: 10.1057/9781137326454

Noh, Jean. 2008. "Warner Bros to release *Dark Knight* on VOD before DVD in Korea." *Screen Daily.com*, 3 December. Accessed 18 February 2013 http://www.screendaily.com/warner-bros-to-release-dark-knight-on-vod-before-dvd-in-korea/4042216.article

Nordenstreng, Kaarle and Varis, Tapio. 1974. *Television traffic – a one-way street? A survey and analysis of the international flow of television programme material.* Paris: UNESCO.

Olsen, Stefanie and Hansen, Evan. 2003. "Disney preps wireless video service." *CNET*, 7 April. Accessed 18 February, 2013 http://news.cnet.com/2100-1025-995846.html

Owen, Rob. 2012. "Netflix and Hulu to unveil original shows for the web." *Pittsburgh Post-Gazette*, 7 February. Accessed 7 February 2012 http://www.courierpress.com/news/2012/feb/07/netflix-and-hulu-unveil-original-shows-web-channel/

Parrack, Dave. 2009a. "YouTube to acquire full-length movies from Sony? From UGC to premium continues." *WebTVWire*, 7 April. Accessed 18 February 2013 http://www.webtvwire.com/youtube-to-acquire-full-length-movies-from-sony-from-ugc-to-premium-continues/

Parrack, Dave. 2009b. "U2 concert is YouTube hit with 10 million live streams | Huge success for Google & Akamai." *WebTVWire.com*, 29 October. Accessed 16 February 2013 http://www.webtvwire.com/u2-concert-is-youtube-hit-with-10-million-live-streams-huge-success-for-google-akamai/

Parrack, Dave. 2010. "Google looks to YouTube as a venue for live sports after Indian Premier League cricket." *WebTVWire.com*, 3 May. Accessed 16 February 2013 http://www.webtvwire.com/google-looks-to-youtube-as-venue-for-live-sports-after-indian-premier-league-cricket/

Perren, Alisa. 2010. "Business as usual: conglomerate-sized challenges for film and television in the digital arena." *Journal of Popular Film & Television* 38 (2): 72–78.

Perren, Alisa and Karen Petruska. 2012. "Big Hollywood, small screens." In *Moving data: the iPhone and the future of media*, edited by Pelle Snickars and Patrick Vonderau, 103–123. New York: Columbia University Press.

Puttnam, David with Watson, Neil. 1998. *Movies and money.* New York: Alfred A. Knopf.

DOI: 10.1057/9781137326454

Ramsaye, Terry. 1986. *A million and one nights: a history of the motion picture through 1925.* Reprinted from 1927. New York: Simon & Schuster.

Rawhiti-Forbes, Troy. 2010. "Online movie library set for the 'killer app.'" *New Zealand Herald,* 9 November. Accessed 19 February 2013 http://www.nzherald.co.nz/movies/news/article.cfm?c_id=200&objectid=10686270

Rayburn, Dan. 2010. "Veoh should be a reminder that execution & focus are more important than vision." *Business Insider,* 13 February. Accessed 14 June 2011 http://www.businessinsider.com/Veoh-bust-should-be-a-reminder-that-execution-and-focus-are-more-important-than-vision-2010-2

Reich, Leonard S. 1992. "Lighting the path to profit: GE's control of the electric lamp industry, 1892–1941." *Business History Review.* 66 (2): 305–335.

Reich, Robert. 2007. *Supercapitalism: the transformation of business, democracy, and everyday life.* New York: Alfred A. Knopf.

Reisinger, Don. 2007. "Will there ever be another MovieBeam?" *Gigaom,* 21 December. Accessed 18 February 2013 http://gigaom.com/2007/12/21/will-there-ever-be-another-moviebeam/

Reuters. 2008. "YouTube to post full-length MGM films." *Reuters,* 10 November. Accessed 14 June 2011 http://www.reuters.com/article/idUSTRE4A90KO20081110

Richmond, Shane. 2012. "Apple 'considering bid for Premier League TV rights.'" *The Telegraph.co.uk,* 4 January. Accessed 4 January 2012 http://www.telegraph.co.uk/technology/apple/8991887/Apple-considering-bid-for-Premier-League-TV-rights.html

Richmond, Will. 2009. "Other analysts waking up to concerns about Hulu's business model." *VideoNuze,* 20 May. Accessed 14 June 2011 http://www.videonuze.com/article/other-analysts-waking-up-to-concerns-about-hulu-s-business-model

Richmond, Will. 2010. "Veoh throws in the towel after $70 million invested." *VideoNuze,* 12 February. Accessed 14 June 2011 http://www.videonuze.com/blogs/?2010-02-12/Veoh-Throws-in-the-Towel-After-70-Million-Invested/&id=2433

Richmond, Will. 2011. "With Next New Networks deal, YouTube evokes cable's early days." *VideoNuze.com,* 9 March. Accessed 16 February 2013 http://www.videonuze.com/article/with-next-new-networks-deal-youtube-evokes-cable-s-early-days/?print=true

DOI: 10.1057/9781137326454

Rick, Christophor. 2009. "80% of Internet users watch online video, worldwide." *ReelSEO*, 6 May. Accessed 14 June 2011 http://www. reelseo.com/80-Internet-users-watch-Online -video-worldwide/

Robischon, Noah. 2000. "Too pooped to pop?" *EW.com*, 9 June. Accessed 18 February 2013 http://www.ew.com/ew/ article/0,,276352,00.html

Roettgers, Janko. 2011. "Where Netflix wants to go next: India, Korea, Japan?" *Gigaom.com*, 2 November. Accessed 22 November 2012 http:// gigaom.com/video/netflix-international-expansion-plans/

Roettgers, Janko. 2012a. "Hulu in'11: $420MM revenue, 1.5M paying subscribers." *Gigaom.com*, 12 January. Accessed 18 February 2013 http://gigaom.com/2012/01/12/hulu-2011-renenue/

Roettgers, Janko. 2012b. "With new channel investments, YouTube becomes even more like TV." *Gigaom.com*, 12 November. Accessed 16 February 2013 http://gigaom.com/video/youtube-original-content-success-rates/

Roller, Emma. 2013. "House of Cards is paying off for Netflix." *Slate*, 21 February. Accessed 25 February 2013 http://www.slate.com/blogs/ moneybox/2013/02/21/house_of_cards_netflix_subscribers_say_the_ series_will_make_them_less_likely.html

Rosoff, Matt and Carlson, Nicholas. 2011. "Guess who made the highest bid for Hulu." *Business Insider*, 27 September. Accessed 16 February 2013 http://articles.businessinsider.com/2011–09–27/ tech/30204790_1_hulu-google-bid-larry-page

Sacks, Danielle. 2011. "How YouTube's global platform is redefining the entertainment business." *FastCompany.com*, 31 January. Accessed 16 February 2013 http://www.fastcompany.com/magazine/152/blown-away.html

Sale, Charles. 2012. "I want! Apple stalk TV deal for Premier League." *Daily Mail.co.uk*, 4 January. Accessed 4 January 2012 http://www. dailymail.co.uk/sport/football/article-2081869/Apple-want-Premier-League-TV-rights-Charles-Sale.html

Sandoval, Greg. 2007. "Blockbuster acquires Movielink." *CNET*, 8 August. Accessed 18 February 2013 http://news.cnet.com/ blockbuster-acquires-movielink/2100–1026_3–6201609.html

Schroeder, Stan. 2008. "MySpace adds videos to its mobile portal." *Mashable.com*, 3 December. Accessed 14 June 2011 http://mashable. com/2008/12/03/myspace-video-streaming-mobile/

DOI: 10.1057/9781137326454

Schumpeter, Joseph A. 1934. *The theory of economic development*. Boston: Harvard University Press.

Screen Digest. 2007. "Google Video drops paid for TV downloads." *Screen Digest. Highbeam Research,* 1 September. Accessed 16 February 2013 http://www.highbeam.com/doc/1G1–179936308.html

Screen Digest. 2008. "Online TV and video audience demand continues to grow but profit evades many players." *Screen Digest,* 11 November. Accessed 14 June 2011 http://www.screendigest.com/press/releases/pr_11_11_2008/view.html

Screen Digest, 2009, 'Movie download market fragments', *Screen Digest,* February 2009.

Scoble, Robert. 2007. "Hi-def independent films online with Jaman." *Classic ScobleShow,* Podtech interview with Gaurav Dhillon and Faisal Galaria, 27 June. Accessed 12 August 2011 http://connectedsocialmedia.com/2931/hi-def-independent-films-online-with-jaman/

Shiels, Maggie. 2011. "YouTube gets serious about movies." *BBC News,* 10 May. Accessed 16 February 2013 http://www.bbc.com/news/technology-13347014

Shey, Tim. 2012. "Kudos to first-ever YouTube partner rewards recipients." *Broadcasting Ourselves. The Official YouTube Blog,* 19 July. Accessed 19 July 2012 http://youtube-global.blogspot.com.au/2012/07/kudos-to-first-ever-youtube-partner.html

Sklar, Robert. 1994. *Movie-made America*. New York: Vintage Books.

Stables, Kate. 2000. "Cyber cinema: September 2000." *The Guardian,* 1 September. Accessed 14 June 2011 www.guardian.co.uk/film/2000/sep/01/cybercinema

Sweney, Mark. 2011. "YouTube to launch 100 new online channels." *The Guardian,* 31 October. Accessed 16 February 2013 http://www.guardian.co.uk/technology/2011/oct/31/youtube-to-launch-tv-channels

Szalai, Georg. 2012a. "YouTube mulls allowing Original Content partners to charge for subscriptions." *The Hollywood Reporter,* 10 October. Accessed 10 October 2012 http://www.hollywoodreporter.com/news/youtube-original-content-subscriptions-charge-abu-dhabi-400912

Szalai, Georg. 2012b. "Taylor Lautner's 'Abduction' first home entertainment release to hit Facebook day-and-date." *The Hollywood Reporter,* 17 January. Accessed 17 January 2012 http://

DOI: 10.1057/9781137326454

www.hollywoodreporter.com/news/twilights-taylor-lautner-%20 abduction-facebook-282652

Szalai, Georg. 2012c. "Netflix, Weinstein Co. unveil multi-year streaming deal for films including 'The Artist.'" *The Hollywood Reporter,* 21 February. Accessed 21 February 2012 http://www.hollywoodreporter. com/news/netflix-weinstein-unveil-multi-year-293111

TBI Vision. 2012a. "Hulu launches new original series." *TBI Vision,* 5 May. Accessed 5 May 2012 http://tbivision.com/article. php?category=5&article=2816

TBI Vision. 2012b. "Netflix to launch in Sweden." *TBI Vision,* 15 May. Accessed 15 May 2012 http://www.tbivision.com/article. php?category=5&article=2863

Thompson, Anne. 2010. "The Auteurs is now MUBI." *Thompson on Hollywood,* 13 May. Accessed 19 February 2013 http://blogs.indiewire. com/thompsononhollywood/the_auteurs_is_now_MUBI

Timmons, Heather. 2010. "Google sees a new role for YouTube: an outlet for live sports." *New York Times,* 2 May. Accessed 16 February 2013 http://www.nytimes.com/2010/05/03/business/media/03cricket. html?_r=1&partner=rss&emc=rss

Tracey, Michael. 1985. "The poisoned chalice? International television and the idea of dominance." *Daedalus* 114 (4): 17–56.

Tyler, Nathan. 2006. "Google to launch Video Marketplace." *Google.com,* 6 January. Accessed 16 February 2013 http://googlepress.blogspot. com.au/2006/01/google-to-launch-video-marketplace_06.html

Variety. 1959. "Think chart on film: LIFE study gives motivation data." *Variety,* 30 December.

Vascellaro, Jessica E., Efrati, Amir, and Smith, Ethan. 2011. "YouTube recasts for new viewers." *Wall Street Journal,* 7 April. Accessed 7 April 2011 http://online.wsj.com/article/SB100014240527487040136045762 47060940913104.html

Vivarelli, Nick. 2012. "YouTube to charge fee for some content." *Variety,* 10 October. Accessed 10 October 2012 http://www.variety.com/ article/VR1118060542

Wallenstein, Andrew. 2011a. "Netflix competition coming in 2012." *Variety,* 28 December. Accessed 28 December 2011 http://www. variety.com/article/VR1118047961

Wallenstein, Andrew. 2011b. "Yahoo dives back into original series." *Variety,* 30 August. Accessed 16 February 2013 http://www.variety. com/article/VR1118041953

DOI: 10.1057/9781137326454

Wallenstein, Andrew. 2011c. "Netflix seals 'House of Cards' deal." *Variety*, 18 March. Accessed 16 February 2013 http://www.variety.com/article/VR1118034117

Wallenstein, Andrew. 2011d. " 'Arrested Development' to return on Netflix." *Variety*, 18 November Accessed 16 February 2013 http://www.variety.com/article/VR1118046367

Wallenstein, Andrew. 2011e. "Netflix gets back in the game." *Variety*, 20 November. Accessed 16 February 2013 http://www.variety.com/article/VR1118046379

Walsh, Mark. 2009. "Report: TV networks should be afraid – very afraid – of Hulu". *Media Post News*, 14 September. Accessed 14 June 2011 www.mediapost.com/publications/?fa=Articles.showArticle&art_aid=113407

Waugh, Rob. 2011. "YouTube to launch 100 TV Channels – each offering 25 hours of shows per day." *Daily Mail*, 31 October. Accessed 16 February 2013 http://www.dailymail.co.uk/sciencetech/article-2055701/YouTube-launch-100-TV-channels – offering-25-hours-shows-day.html

Wasko, Janet. 1994. *Hollywood in the information age: beyond the silver screen*. Cambridge: Polity Press.

Wei, William. 2010. "Meet the YouTube stars making $100,000 plus per year." *Business Insider*, 19 August. Accessed 12 February 2013 http://www.businessinsider.com/meet-the-richest-independent-youtube-stars-2010–8?op=1#ixzz2LxMopyjr

White, Charlie. 2011. "Apple considering Hulu purchase?" *CNN*, 22 July. Accessed 16 February 2012 http://edition.cnn.com/2011/TECH/web/07/22/apple.buy.hulu.mashable/index.html

Wingfield, Nick and Schneider, Sam. 2011. "Netflix seals deal for original series." *The Wall Street Journal*, 21 March. Accessed 27 November 2012 http://online.wsj.com/article/SB10001424052748703512404576208972975699708.html

Wu, Tim 2010. *The master switch: the rise and fall of information empires*. Chicago: University of Chicago Press.

YouTube. 2012. "A 'Next' step for YouTube nonprofits." *Broadcasting Ourselves;) The Official YouTube Blog*, 17 February. Accessed 1 February 2013 http://youtube-global.blogspot.com.au/2012/02/next-step-for-youtube-nonprofits.html

Yu, Xi. 2012. "Sohu, Tencent and iQiyi cooperate on video copyrights." *Global Times*, 25 April. Accessed 26 February 2013 http://www.

DOI: 10.1057/9781137326454

globaltimes.cn/NEWS/tabid/99/ID/706498/Sohu-Tencent-and-iQiyi-cooperate-on-video-copyrights.aspx

Zhao, Jing and Keane, Michael. Forthcoming 2013. "Between formal and informal: the shakeout in China's online video industry." *Media Culture & Society.*

Zhu, Ying. 2012. *Two billion eyes: the story of CCTV.* New York: The New Press.

Zibreg, Christian. 2011. "Google's new multi-billion market: Hollywood entertainment." *9to5Google.com* , 13 September. Accessed 22 February 2013 http://9to5google.com/2011/09/13/googles-new-65-billion-market-hollywood-entertainment/

Zjawinski, Sonia. 2009. "Streaming hard-to-find films for cinephiles." *Wired*, 22 May. Accessed 18 February 2013 from http://www.wired.com/entertainment/hollywood/magazine/17–06/pl_screen

Zukor, Adolph with Kramer, Dale. 1953. *The public is never wrong.* New York: G. P. Puttnam's Sons.

DOI: 10.1057/9781137326454

Index

DOI: 10.1057/9781137326454

DOI: 10.1057/9781137326454

DOI: 10.1057/9781137326454

DOI: 10.1057/9781137326454

DOI: 10.1057/9781137326454

CPSIA information can be obtained at www.ICGtesting.com
Printed in the USA
BVOW03*1602020813

327507BV00002B/6/P